Four in the Fifties
SEVEN IN THE SIXTIES

BY JENNY HENDERSON

ACKNOWLEDGEMENTS

My thanks, first and foremost, go to both my parents for giving me such a happy childhood
to write about. Other children are not so fortunate, so part of the proceeds from
book sales will go to the BBC's Children in Need Appeal.

For some of my illustrations I needed help in various ways – so thanks go to:

My father for keeping a wonderful family slide collection.
It was invaluable for this book as it filled in many of my memory lapses.

The owners of an old postcard of Chelmsford Bus Station
as it provided the inspiration for my illustration 'Under the Bridge'.

MiAC (Malvern Industrial Archaeological Circle) who kindly provided
technical details for steam engine illustrations.

Four in the Fifties
SEVEN IN THE SIXTIES

Pictures from My Childhood

BY JENNY HENDERSON

Designed and produced by
Inkwell Media Limited
274 Richmond Road
London E8 3QW
Email: enquiries@inkwellmedia.co.uk

ISBN 978-0-9560859-7-9
Printed in India

Jenny Henderson has also written and illustrated
Little Green Shoots about teaching in the Cotswolds
of the 1970s.

inkwell
m e d i a is a publishing company that creates affordable custom-made
books and calendars for schools and organisations – or for individual
authors and artists. We specialise in short print-runs.

If you are interested in publishing a book of short stories, poetry or
recipes – or in creating a book for your community or for fundraising –
please contact us through our website (**www.inkwellmedia.co.uk**).

HOW TO ORDER PRINTS

All the illustrations in this book are available to purchase as
prints. Please refer to the list on pages 6–7 and email me at
jennys.art@hotmail.co.uk or visit **www.jennysart.co.uk**
for my contact details so that I can discuss your order
personally – *Jenny Henderson*.

Introduction

CHILDHOOD MEMORIES are strange creatures. They imprint themselves silently into sunken depths, waiting to be startled and woken by unknown visitors from the future. In half wakefulness they twist and twirl in uncertain meandering streams with unpainted wisps and whirls of white water.

Those are my pictures.

The words are childhood memories and so are spoken in the voice of a child. I wrote some of the words when I was only four years old and some when I was a bit older and could 'spel betta'. The rest were inspired by a visit to a museum in a Norfolk windmill, where I was quite taken aback by the realisation that the ancient exhibits were simply the things I grew up with ...

Those are my stories.

The first home I describe could have been ANY town in the east of England but I called it 'Chumsfod'. Then we moved out west but that wasn't at all like any other town. I called it 'Mollvan'.

All living 'frens 'n' relashuns' mentioned have been given new names – I hope they like them. And I hope you will forgive my occasional spelling and grammar mistakes because, after all, I WAS only a Silly Little Girl.

This is my book.

ILLUSTRATIONS
Scent to send you home

What made me look back and paint these scenes?

I think it all began with a wave of wallflower scent that floated away with me back down rainbow roads of time until I couldn't go back any further. All I could do was paint my way forwards again.

It was my first home that smelt of wallflowers – and freshly cut grass. A cool eveningy, free-time smell of no-school and no-early-to-bed. My growing-up home was a deep apple-blossom-pink and rich emerald grass smell, so different to the dry corn-ripening east coast smell with its tingle-down-the-spine holidayness.

My grandparents' homes smelt of holidays too but had their own special smells as well. Granny's house smelt of polished wood, clean sheets and roses where sticky hands were washed with sweet-scented soap. But Grandma Georgie's home smelt best of all. Its smells were all mixed up – white jasmine, cigary uncles, Grandma's cuddly cotton nightdress and the crisp linen sheets in her huge brass bed; of lazy days, lemon-balm and love.

All illustrations are available to purchase as giclée prints. Please contact me by e-mail so that I can discuss your order personally.

jennys.art@hotmail.co.uk

So, here are my scented scenes:

Four in
the Fifties

When We Three Became Four

"Look at the clouds! Aren't they moving fast today?"
I wanted to look at the clouds just in case I missed anything really interesting but at the same time I was really busy sailing my sailing ship and the sea was very rough so I had to hold on tight. Curiosity in the end overwhelmed my seafaring tendencies and I crawled out of my Top-Sail Schooner, which was a small gate-legged table in the bay window, banging my head on the folded-down table-top (my sail). Mummy held me tight against her soft cotton-aproned tight tummy and wiped my tears away.

"Daddy's coming home to play with you soon," she said and when he did she went upstairs with the nice lady in the blue dress and the nice doctor with his scary black bag. That afternoon Daddy and I made a little stool out of an old piece of oak which he'd been keeping in the garage. We left lots of shavings and sawdust on the front room carpet but Daddy said it was all right that day. We sand-papered the oak top until it was silky smooth and soft to touch but then I wasn't allowed to touch it any more because it was painted with some sticky, smelly stuff that looked like treacle and MUSTN'T BE TOUCHED until Wednesday. By Wednesday I had a little baby sister and the Three of us became Four.

My bedroom until then had been the little room over the front door. After Three became Four, I had the big back room where the sun beamed through in the morning. Daddy had finished the stool but still didn't go back to work, so he painted my walls pale green and the wooden chest of drawers and cupboard pink. Then, we got out the big copper boiler and made the white curtains that went in white come out pink. That's how I got my apple-blossom bedroom. I will tell you another time about the little adventure I had with the windows behind those pretty pink curtains.

My House

We lived in a pretty house, with a black-and-cream timbered gable over the big bay windows which had little oblong leaded lights. Our house was joined to another house – just the same but opposite way round – so their front door was the wrong side and when you went in you couldn't find the front room. There were other houses just like these along our short road. Daddy said they were built between the wars. I didn't understand this because the only thing I could see between them was a wide pebbly road. To begin with, all the houses matched, being painted a smart, respectable black and cream. Then one man painted his brown, which Daddy said was "just about acceptable" because he liked Mr Lincoln. Another man painted his green which was "fairly favourable" as the paint was going cheap and they were old people – but THEN one man painted his house a really shiny bright red! Daddy wasn't "quite sure" about that man after that. I liked it.

All our houses had big front gardens with a low wall and a black metal chain hanging between painted posts which matched the house colour. We had three golden laburnums by our front wall that glowed like fires in the afternoon sun. The back gardens were full of flowers and shrubs and long enough to run in as fast as you possibly could before your side ached. Everyone had a vegetable plot hidden behind the pretty bit and some people kept chickens too. Right at the bottom of the gardens on our side was a sunken bit like a low valley and this was kept wild with trees and bushes and the grass was cut long instead of short. Here I had my swing, Mummy had her spidery summer-house and Daddy had his compost heap. In the spring all the little white petals of the May trees would fall, floating like little fairy wings onto the emerald grass below – so there really were fairies at the bottom of our garden. There were ugly little grey things as well under the stones that curled up in a ball when you picked them up, just like the Big Boys' leather football. I loved playing in my garden 'bestest' of all and always cried when it rained and I had to stay in.

We lived in the last road EVER. It was the last road of town before the fields started. Our road wasn't "made up". Well, it was "made up" but it was made up of pebbles and potholes and thick brown bubbly puddles that grew when it rained. Mummy said that this made it a very safe place to live because the cars had to go very slowly.

Our road was quiet, not just because it was the last road ever but also because it went nowhere, dying out just before the buttercup fields and the flat green river valley with its clay pits. The clay pit right at the end of our road was the deepest hole in the whole world – and

the scariest. It was scarier even than the grizzly bear that could "hug-you-tight-with-all-his-might-till-you-were-flat-as-a-tyre-without-air". Or the war.

If you were brave enough to walk round the edge of this scary deep pit, holding Daddy's hand VERY tightly, a sandy track led down to the slow bottle-green river crossed by a flat wooden bridge with low metal railings. Here were the remains of a waterwheel in an old mill where naughty boys had thrown stones through the little window-panes. Daddy said the river drove the wheels that once made bricks there and the pit was the hole they dug the clay from. Whatever the case, this was a very good place to fish for minnows because they liked the freshly bubbled water that rushed over the weir and slowed down by the warm, sandy shore. We were only ever allowed to go fishing with A Grown-up. That was usually my daddy because he knew how to do all those sorts of things.

In contrast to the scary pits and the dark mill, everything at home felt safe and comforting. Nothing nasty or unexpected (apart from

waiting he noisily raked out the ashes from the front room fire and put them in the grey bucket. At this very exact point each morning I would say,

"What's today?" and he would answer,

"Today is today," so I had to ask again until he said,

"Monday," or "Friday."

Consequently, I thought that there actually was a day of the week called 'Today' and that it sat somewhere between Tuesday and Thursday.

After making up the front room fire, using another noisy metal thing he riddled out the speckledy blue kitchen stove which stood on bendy metal things (like Aunty Vi's legs) and he put on some more coke out of the tall, black coal-scuttle. Sometimes the stove went out in the night and Daddy had to light it with the gas poker which had a scary roaring noise – but if you hid behind the door you could still see the pretty blue and yellow flames turn the coke bright red again.

When the kettle whistled and blew out steam, he poured a little hot water into the teapot to warm it up then tipped it out again. Into the green teapot he put three silver spoonfuls of tea from the silver tea-caddy and the boiling water went on top with a frothy, floppity noise until it was full. Then you had to leave it for four whole minutes before you could stir it but it didn't seem a long time because I sat on the table and had a glass of milk while we listened to some music on the wireless.

After Mummy had drunk her tea up in bed we had breakfast in the

Three becoming Four) ever seemed to happen and home had a warm reassuring routine.

We got up at seven o'clock. First Daddy and I went downstairs and he lit the gas cooker with the clicky handle at the side and the blue flame shot out of its little oblong windows. When the blue flame lost its yellow bits he filled the kettle and put it on to boil. While he was green dining room where the long green flowery curtains hugged the French windows. In the summer they were always open letting in the golden morning sun. We had Cornflakes from a huge cockerel's box with 'Orbran' on top. In winter we had 'podge with trickle' on top. After, we had 'baco, negg and frybread'. Then Daddy had Olde English grown-ups' marmalade with horrid hard bits of orange peel in but I had jelly marmalade on toast. Mummy didn't have time for marmalade as she was doing the toast. Mummy often burnt the toast because she cooked it under the gas grill and it was too low down for her to watch it without bending down. It was just the right height for me though, and I would gaze in a haze at the soft blue hue until the glowing yellow gas flames turned the grey metal grill into burnished red light. I loved those colours. Breakfast was always the same. Whatever day it was.

After breakfast Mummy washed up whilst Daddy and I cleaned

our teeth in the white tiled bathroom. The tiles had a little black pattern running all round the middle telling me how much I had grown in the night. I had Punch and Judy strawberry toothpaste in a tiny tube but Daddy had some horrid-smelling green stuff in a huge fat tube. After doing my teeth I would watch him shave. First, he sharpened the razor by flick-flacking it up and down a red mat in an oblong metal tray but the best bit was wetting the soft white-tipped bristles of the short-handled brush and sloshing it round the little white soap tin until it made a sloppity white snow which he painted all over his face. The scraping it off bit wasn't so interesting so I usually left then or crept round to have a look at the scar on his back that he got in the war. The scar didn't bother me because I assumed everyone's Daddy had a scar from the war. I was afraid of the war though, even if it HAD ended before I was born.

Monday was Washing Day

After Daddy had gone to work, Mummy put on her paisley housecoat and the housekeeping routine began. Washing-up time was my cue to go out into the garden and play but Mondays in the kitchen were a little more enticing as the huge linen copper came out and into the boiling hot steam went all the white sheets and towels poked down into the soapy white Lux suds with the well-worn wash-stick. The best bit was when Mummy put some bright-blue stuff in and made the water blue but the sheets still came out white. That was really puzzling because even at three-and-a-half years old, I knew there was no such thing as magic. The next bit was a very dangerous bit because all the boiling hot steamy sheets had to be picked up with a huge pair of washing tongs and be squeezed through the mangle. They were too

hot to touch and the soapy steam went up my nose and tingled. I wasn't allowed to talk while this was happening and NEVER EVER allowed to put my fingers anywhere near because a terrible thing had happened to an aunt in a mangle.

When Three became Four the sheets all got sent away to be washed at the laundry because washing them at home was "too much hard work with a baby". They came back in a cream van but they weren't very clean because there was black writing on the edges. Mummy said it was a 'laundry mark'. I thought they weren't very good at washing if they made marks on your laundry and was pleased when normality finally returned. The black marks on the edge of my sheets never came out though.

One day Mummy got a present in a huge cardboard box which was really exciting at first but very disappointing when it was opened. It wasn't a two-wheeled red bike. It was a new cream washing machine with its own joined-on mangle on top which worked by 'lectric'. The clothes went in the top under a little blue lid and the 'lectric' drove a little fluted disc from side to side with a vrum-vrum noise. All the soapy washing went magically through the mangles without you having to wind anything, then had to go in the sink to be rinsed, then mangled again. The mangled clothes landed

in a blue tray at the back which was cleverly the upturned lid of the machine so when all the washing was done you could fold it all up small again and wheel the machine back into a much smaller space than the huge linen copper and old mangle took up.

After our old mangle was retired to the garage, I crept in and very naughtily pressed my finger into the black gap between the wooden rollers and began to turn the huge metal handle – just to see if it really was as dangerous as I'd been told. I couldn't really see what all the fuss was about. When it started to hurt I just turned the big metal handle the other way and out rolled my rather pale, slightly flatter finger.

The mangle handle got tied securely to the mangle after that little experiment.

We had our main meal at midday when Daddy came back from work for his dinner except on Wednesdays. Monday's dinner was cold meat and mashed potatoes with greens in but I didn't ever eat the brown pickle because it looked like something Mrs Emery's cat did in the cat tray in her kitchen. After dinner I had a rest because it was "good for you". I climbed into the Parker Knoll wing chair and put my ear right up to the gold bit on the wireless to listen to *Listen with Mother* but My Mother listened in the kitchen and did the washing-up. I could have listened in the kitchen too because Daddy had fixed a

little varnished box with a green curtained front onto a long twisted wire that joined the back of the wireless. That meant you could hear it in the kitchen too and Mummy could work while *Music While You Work* played music while she worked. But I wanted my ear right up close in case I missed anything.

The only other programme Mummy liked was 'Mrs Dalesdyree'. 'Mrs Dalesdyree' was a nice lady with a very nice voice but she didn't do anything, except say, "Oh hello, Jim dear," every time her husband came home. And Jim was always saying, "Hello Mother-in-law," to a very squeaky old lady. That wasn't a very good story.

My programme was much better. First, a nice lady said, "Hello Children," then she sang a nursery rhyme with a man's voice that wasn't so nice. Then the really exciting bit was the story, which was always a different one each day but it never lasted long enough and I had to listen to another nursery rhyme, which I already knew. Sometimes the lady would ask something in a silly, slow voice and then sing the rhyme all over again when they COULD have made the story last longer. My 'bestest' music programme was *Children's Favourites* because Uncle Mac's voice was soft and kind and he played the music that children had actually asked for. He hardly ever played the same music again and again.

Our wireless was a long varnished box in two sections. One bit was where the sound came out and was a bit scary because if you looked closely behind the gold metal there was a deep dark hole. The other side was a black glassy bit that lit up and there were four lines going down with VERY big numbers for Home, Light, Third and World with lots of place names on. I could read all the names except Luxembourg. Some of the names were warm and friendly, like London. But I was afraid of Berlin because it had something to do with the war and I didn't want another war to happen.

When I was a bit older I was allowed to watch *Watch with Mother* and this time Mother did watch too because the washing-up was done by then. Monday though, was *Picture Box* and I didn't like that so I played in the garden.

Tuesday was Polishing and Ironing

I helped for a little while with the polishing but rubbing it off with the yellow duster was the only bit I liked because yellow was my favourite colour. The first bit was done with a dirty grey duster that you wiped around the polish in a wide round tin that smelt of lavender. And bees.

All the wooden furniture and all the wooden legs of the cloth furniture had to be done and then all the floorboards round the edge of the carpets. We had a lot of wooden stuff so I went out to play in the garden before we'd finished. Then I could watch all the windows being made pink with Windowleen so I couldn't see in, until the other yellow duster polished them shiny again. A man on a ladder with a bucket did the outsides of the windows and I ran right to the bottom of the garden when he came because his voice was too deep.

Tuesday dinner was Shepherd's Pie made from the last bit of Sunday Lunch or sausages if the Sunday Lunch was chicken. Then *Andy Pandy* came on. Mummy watched this too while she did the ironing in the front room with a hot and dangerous thing she called a 'flat'. I supposed it was called that because it made the clothes flat. I wasn't allowed near the flat, but when the ironing board was folded up it was my sailing boat and I sailed far away across the sea in it and got home just in time for tea.

Wednesday was Hoovering

I was afraid of our Hoover. Mostly I was afraid of the loud noise and the dusty blue bag that swelled up when it breathed but, even worse, it had a huge black mouth at the front of its silver face which Mummy kept having to open when "it went fut" or the belt came off. I think its name was 'Gec' because it was written on its forehead. It always ran around the carpets in a hurry and banged its black plastic wheels into things all the time and Mummy would shout,

"Mind out of the way please, I have to go to the shop soon, I'm in a hurry!"

So hoovering was always a rather stressful event. It still is today.

When it was finished and put back in the cupboard where it couldn't bite me, we sat at the table in blissful peace and quiet and quickly wrote The List. The List had to be taken up the road to The Corner Shop.

First, my baby sister was put into the big black pram with its big cloth hood. The shiny body of the pram sat on big squidgy springs which you must NEVER put your fingers near or they would get cut off. Underneath were four wheels with shiny silver spokes, two giant ones near the handle and two smaller ones at the front and they had solid white tyres like my tricycle's. The pram was really fun to push because it went really fast and rocked over the bumps with its bouncy springs. Unfortunately I was too small to see where I was going over the high hood. If it was a nice day we walked down the road and took the path over the fields and passed the timber yard

with the fascinating little crane like a cable-car. We stopped going that way after I refused to leave it until it had emptied "just one more load" and the shop had shut for half day closing even though we had run all the rest of the way, over the red brick bridge and across the park under the chestnut trees.

Inside the Corner Shop there was a man who sliced the bacon up however you wanted it – thick, thin or medium – on a swirling silver wheel that screamed as it cut. I did wonder whether it might be the bacon squealing. The bacon-cutter man only had two fingers.

We left The List at the shop and took the bacon home to the meat-safe in the pantry so it stayed fresh. Sometimes we went to get

fish from the fishmongers and sometimes the lady brought it to our house because she lived over the road and was Mummy's best friend. The fish went in the meat-safe in the pantry too. The pantry had a special window made out of wire mesh instead of glass and the wind blew cold on your face when you peered through the holes. The meat-safe had the same window. We bought soap at a broom shop – green for the kitchen, white for the bathroom – and little white flakes for clothes-washing. We didn't buy greens from the greengrocers because Daddy knew all about how to grow all those green things but we did buy oranges and apples to go on our little wooden fruit-stand. All this shopping went on the wire mesh tray under the pram. On the way home I was allowed on the swings but not too high because the little wooden seat didn't have any sides. Sometimes the metal chains were too cold to hold and I had to hold on with my inside-elbows. When we got home it was long past dinner-time so I had scrambled egg "cos it's quick" and watched *Bill and Ben*.

On Thursday the Shopping Came
(with my sweets)

Next day all the things on The List came to our house in a big card-board box in a little white van. I don't know why we had to write a list because the box always had the same things in, always packed in their very own places. First came the cockerel's giant packet of Cornflakes and the smaller 'Orbran' next to it, then a red box of Quaker Oats with a scary old lady's face on. Next to them, a red bag and a blue bag of McDougals flour and a red bag and a blue bag of Tate & Lyle sugar and one dark brown sugar, one packet of currants and one of sultanas and suet, rice and semolina. Beside these packets were red sauce, brown sauce, Worcester Sauce and Heinz salad cream then the jars of Robertson's red jam, lemon curd, Daddy's horrid chunky marmalade and my delicious jelly marmalade. Then came the tins: Golden Syrup (which I thought was called 'trickle' cos it did) with the picture of the sad but scary lion on the green and gold swirly-patterned tin, tinned fruit-salad, baby oranges and peaches with tinned milk to go on them and lastly the soft stuff – a roll of butter, in a greased paper packet, a blue box of lard and a huge slab of cheese, wrapped up in two layers of greaseproof paper. If I was very lucky there might also be a tiny white bag with a screwed-up top containing jelly-babies or white chocolate drops with crunchy little beads on. I always ate the whole packet all at once and then I couldn't eat all my dinner up which was 'Steak and Kiggly'. I only

ate the soft 'kiggly' and dumpling and left the chewy steak. After dinner, *Rag, Tag and Bobtail* came on.

Other things were delivered to the house every day – except the coal which came a long time apart. That came on a big dirty green lorry driven by men with very dirty black faces. When they got out of the lorry they put on black leather waist-coats with metal studs all down the back so the lumpy bags of coal wouldn't hurt. They walked backwards to the lorry sides and picked up the black sacks with two hands behind their shoulders and then

had to lean a long way forwards and walk quickly all the way round to the coal store at the back next to the pantry, looking rather cross. When they tipped all the coal out of the bag it sounded like thunder. They only smiled and stood upright when they were on the way back and then their teeth would look really white and their lips really red and scary against their coal-black faces. I was a little afraid of these big coalmen. But I did like the Teddy Bear Coalman in my 'bestest' storybook.

The baker was very nice because he smiled ALL the time. He brought the bread to the back door in a huge square basket with a looped handle. There was every sort of bread you could imagine, long sticks, twisty sticks, cottage loaves, currant loaves, plaited loaves, round loaves and square loaves. He showed us every single loaf but we always had the same. "One large white and one small brown, please," Mummy said and handed over the big brown pennies.

My favourite deliveryman was the milkman because he had a black and white horse. I loved that horse even though he did reach over our front wall and eat Daddy's wallflowers. The horse wore a collar made of thick brown leather with two shiny brass bits at the top that the reins ran through. On his face he had a thick-strapped harness and nasty black eye-guards so he could only see straight ahead. Attached to his collar were two chains, on which hung the green wooden shafts of the milk-float. The float was decorated in an elegant cream and green pattern and had a green roof with a fluted edge

As we were the last road ever, when the horse got to the end of the road all the milk bottles on board were empty ones and his day's work was ended so he was given a bag of oats to eat from a nosebag, whilst the milkman sat on his high seat and ate his sandwiches. When they'd both finished the milkman would shout, "Gee up Neddy!" and the horse would turn the milk-float all the way round, making the green wooden wheels draw triangle patterns in the gravel.

covering the crates of milk, the egg boxes and the little bottles of orange syrup that children got "after the war". The milkman had a little springy metal step to climb up onto his worn wooden seat and a long, green, angled board to rest his feet on. He leant against the cream back of the float and a little bit of its roof came over his head to protect him from the rain. How I wanted to be that milkman. The horse was a very, very clever horse. Without being told, it would walk on to the next house when the man dropped off the full bottles and picked up the empty milk bottles and it knew exactly where to stop. It knew especially where to stop by our house so it could reach the wallflowers without any extra steps and it always ate the evidence before the milkman returned. We always had two silver-topped pints for Mummy and Daddy, one red-topped pint for me, a little bottle of orange syrup each day, with two dozen eggs once a week.

Then it would toss its head up and shake its white mane before trotting gleefully back along the road lifting its feathery feet high up in the air and jangling all the empty glass bottles in their crates.

Friday was Fish and Chips

Friday was a stressful sort of day because a great deal of fuss was made by Mummy – just over cooking the fish and chips lunch. First of all, before Daddy went to work, he would put on his big black rubber boots and dig up the potatoes. Then there was a lot of fuss as Mummy scrubbed and peeled them in the white 'porslin' sink and cross things were said and spluttered about the slugs and the bad bits you had to gouge out with the end bit of the peeler. Then the clean yellow potatoes were cut into long pieces and "put to rest" and there was a brief, happy respite as we trotted down the garden to put the peelings on the compost heap. Then the muttering and spluttering began again when Mummy unwrapped the fish from its soggy greaseproof paper. From then on I was not allowed to leave any doors open in case the fishy smell escaped from the kitchen and "crept all over the house". First the fish was covered in flour and salt and pepper then Mummy always did a peculiar thing. She got a large paisley scarf and wrapped it right around her head, tying it like a turban and she buttoned her housecoat right up tight to her chin.

After that it was time to heat the hard white fat in the chip-pan until it magically turned to clear liquid and the rested, drowned potato sticks were taken out of the water and dried in a tea-towel, just like cups and saucers, before being tipped into the hot fat with a sizzle and a squelch of steam. I was allowed to watch but only sitting at the very far end of the table, right away from the gas-stove, and I had to "not talk to me now because I have two things to watch," as the floury fish went into the shallower pan.

When the three plates of fish and chips were finally plated up they had to be taken very quickly through to the dining room and the doors firmly shut again "to catch the fishy smells". I had red sauce and Daddy had brown. Mummy always ate her fish with a slightly turned-up nose and then said, "I don't really think I like fish very much". I thought that it was rather a lot of effort to go to if you didn't even like fish.

She kept her hair wrapped in the turban right up until *The Woodentops* had finished.

Tea-times and the afternoons preceding were altogether far more relaxed because the main housework was done and "other little jobs" could be done at their own leisurely pace. Tea had much more stuff to lay on the table but with most of the cooking having been done in the mornings Mummy said there was no pressure of "getting it all done on time". First, a nice crisp tablecloth went on the drop-leaf oak table and then the pale green cups and saucers and small green plates, each with a small bone-handled knife. There was sugar in the silver bowl, milk in the big jug with the green teapot waiting in the kitchen by the kettle, jam in the precious Wedgwood dish, grated cheese in a pudding bowl, salad and red fruit from the garden in summer or tinned fruit in the winter. There was always a cake. I was allowed to make a sponge because with the same weight of butter, sugar eggs and flour, if I helped myself to a teeny bit of mixture it wouldn't matter. Sponge-cake could have other fillings or flavours such

as chocolate, coffee or orange to "make a change from jam". Mummy had to make the flapjacks or ginger biscuits on her own because of the TOO HOT melted butter that was VERY DANGEROUS.

Then the fun bit was back in the kitchen, cutting the bread with the bone-handled knife on the scarred breadboard (both of which I have to this day) and spreading it with butter warmed under the red gas grill. All the bread was piled onto a big dinner plate and set on the table. With the kettle already boiled and left to simmer, Mummy got changed out of her housecoat and put on "something nice," usually with her cameo necklace, to wait by the fire until Daddy got home and the boiling water from the kettle went floppiting onto the tea-leaves and the tea-pot was dressed warmly in its tea-cosy. Tea-time too was cosy and warm and safe.

Only occasionally did Mummy do any spluttering about. That was when boiled eggs were on the menu and Daddy was a bit late, making them too hard to get your bread fingers into. Worse STILL than being late was if Daddy brought kippers home for tea and yellow fish for me – as a special treat. This was far worse than the fish and chips rigmarole, requiring Mummy to wear all her old clothes and a DOUBLE turban, and quite a lot more muttering and spluttering was involved. The whole house had to be aired and cleaned the following day to blow away "that stinking fish".

"I don't think Mummy likes fish," I said to Daddy behind the tightly closed kitchen door, as he washed up the little white enamel fish dish with the blue edge and Mummy had a bath and washed her hair upstairs.

I spent the whole of my evenings trying to find ways of delaying bedtime. They never seemed to work. First, I would sit right in front of the fire and gaze into the hazy red caves between the coals and watch the flames meander up the black chimney. When Daddy put on more coals and made the fire black, I couldn't POSSIBLY go to bed until the fire went yellow again because that was my favourite colour. Then I would HAVE to listen to Cy Grant play his guitar and sing on the television because it was always my favourite song – whatever it was. Then I HAD to wait until Cliff Michelmore said, "The Next Tonight's Tomorrow Night" – because of course it would be, silly man – but then I was too tired to think of any more reasons to stay awake so I went up to my apple-blossom bedroom and climbed into my covered wagon and the horses rocked me to sleep as they pioneered the prairies.

Saturday and Sunday

Weekends also had their routines that varied with the seasons and the weather but weekends always had a special feel of freedom. Daddy still had to go to work but only on Saturday morning and he was allowed to wear his sports jacket. It was cream colour with a dark-brown dogstooth check and brown leather patches on the elbows. It was not nice to touch because it was woolly and itchy.

In the winter we had steak for Saturday lunch because Daddy played hockey and "needed his strength". I thought it was horrid and chewy. Daddy packed all his green and white hockey clothes, boots and two hockey sticks (because one often broke) into a long faded green bag with a brown leather handle and buckled straps. He put the bag in the boot of our little black Austin then drove to the County Ground. Mummy and I, with the pram, used to walk all the way up to the County Ground "to catch the second half" whatever that was – I don't know if we ever caught it. All I knew was that it was a long way for little legs to walk. It was fun to begin with, especially because after you'd walked up into town under all the sunshades of the little shops, you had to walk

under the dark red railway bridge. It was the main London line so it was always very busy and because you could see it for a long while before you got there, you would always be able to see two or three trains and the big sooty black steam engines always stopped right on top of the bridge with their carriages behind them at the station. They pulled off with a whistle *Fooo, Fooo* and then first one slow and three little chuffs, *CHUFF chuf chuf chuf*. Then four slow ones, *CHUFFF, CHUFFF, CHUFFF, CHUFFF,* as it began to move and the rods climbed round the huge oily wheels. Then it got better at it and began to move faster *CHUFF, CHUFF, CHUFF, CHUFF,* until the chuffs all went together in a *Ch, Ch, Ch, Ch, Ch, Ch, Ch, Ch* and the red carriages behind started to go *Te-dum Te-dah, Te-dum Te-dah* and the whole train went over the hundreds of brick arches on its way to London shrouded in billowing steam and sooty smoke. I loved steam engines almost as much as horses. At night I could hear the trains chuffing along that great long viaduct whose enormous arches looped across the river and the ponds in the park.

Once Daddy and I stopped by some railway railings to watch a steam engine on a turntable. I gripped hard to the railings, poking my head through the gap. It was a huge engine

and was taking an unbearably long time to get itself in position on the turntable so Daddy said it was time to go. I refused to leave, gripping like a vice with a hand on each railing and screaming, "NO, NO, I won't GO!" Daddy had to use two of his big hands to prise each one of mine open and when he started on the next hand I swiftly welded the first hand back on. This went on for several minutes until the steam engine had been turned right round on the turntable and disappeared and a little crowd of tut-tutting onlookers had gathered and frowned at Daddy. "I've never been so embarrassed in all my life!" Daddy fumed.

My usually calm Daddy related this to ALL my relations that he met in turn throughout the year. I felt quite justified and remained so, despite all the gasps and sighs – after all it was the biggest steam engine EVER.

After the railway bridge the proper big shops began, like the busy 'Woolwuffs' and 'Mark Suspender' that you had to be very careful not to get lost in and so HOLD ON TIGHT. Then there was a stone bridge with round balustrades over a river and then a grey cathedral

and this was where my little legs began to get tired. Sometimes I was allowed to sit on the pram but had to mind not to suffocate my little sister, like the cat 'nexdoor' tried to do.

Eventually we went down a lane of dark trees beside a grey hospital and there was my daddy playing hockey. I thought they were very lucky to have a hospital close by because someone was always getting hit on the head in the game. As it began to get dark, the yellow lights came on in the hospital windows and you could see the nurses rushing around. You knew they were nurses because nurses always walked quickly and made their uniforms sing a crisp, clean song.

We always sat outside the wooden pavilion where the warmth blew out from its open doors with a golden yellow light. It smelt of ham sandwiches and beer, with squashed grass and muddy boards because they always played on a grass pitch. When the game finished all the men put on lumpy cream jumpers that looked like bread sauce and they went into the pavilion with deep, loud, laughy voices that made my bones hum. That scared me, so Daddy used to take us home in the car. Then he went

back for his beer and ham sandwiches. It wasn't only people who played hockey who liked sandwiches because I once asked Uncle Jack what Father Christmas had brought him and he said, "…a sand wedge because he knows I like playing golf".
I felt sorry for him, only getting a sandwich for Christmas.

Back home we had a much better tea than the shouty hockey men in that noisy pavilion did because we toasted our bread and crumpets on the yellow front room fire. We always forgot to move the butter before it "all ran-away-to-nothing" because we were too busy waiting for the man on the television who read out the football results, to say, "Hamilton Academicals" which was a really, really funny thing to say.

SUNday WAS always a sunny day usually spent in the garden. Daddy dug the vegetable garden in the winter and we collected frosted sprouts and cabbages that made your hands wet and tingly. He mowed the lawn in summer with his blue cylinder mower, tipping the grass cuttings between the raspberry rows – and that made my running track. At Coffee Time some of the neighbours would come round or we went to their house but only just long enough for a chat because everyone had "things to do".

Sometimes when the "things to do" needed it, ALL the neighbours would help. One day there was a terrible crash of broken glass that was Mr Slater's guttering falling into his French Windows. Everyone said it was because he "didn't maintain his property properly", but everyone helped him clear up and fix them all the same.

When Mr Lincoln came to us he had coffee like the other grown-ups but when we went to his, he had horrible brown stuff that smelt of stew gravy and he slurped it with a very rude bubbling sound. I wasn't allowed to do that. His face was wrinkled with deep jaggety lines just like his huge grey leather gardening boots with the giant tongues that you didn't go near in case they ate you.

Mr and Mrs Lincoln were as old as my grandparents and because we didn't see my grandmas and grandads 'cept' on holidays, Mummy liked to take The Lincolns "out for the day" instead. We always took them to 'Haybree Bason', even though they found it quite hard to walk across the top of the scary lock-gates AND-NOT-LOOK-DOWN, because they liked to walk along the flat sea wall and breathe in the sea air. Sometimes the lock-gates were open and you couldn't cross over the deep water so we walked the other way. When we stopped for our picnic the sea sometimes came right up to the walls and sometimes went out and left squelchy grey mud that you MUSTN'T stand on or you'd SINK UP TO YOUR NECK and get stuck there – forever and ever.

"Can't we go round to that sandy bit?" I always asked, gazing longingly at crowds of people having fun on a yellow beach far round the bay. But The Lincolns couldn't walk that far and said it was "not a very nice place anyway" with a screwed-up nose, which meant the people there were doing things that we would never do. I never found out what those things were. "Our" end was full of little black weatherboard huts, tarred black boats with thick dark ropes and curled up rust-red sails. There were little sailing boats too whose masts and rigging chinked in the breeze and whose little white sails flapped like my new pink curtains – so it was still quite fun.

On ordinary Sundays with no picnic, we had garden vegetables with a big roast but had to leave half the meat for leftovers in the week. Mummy made little batter puddings and whilst I battered the batter Daddy always said a rhyme. I didn't understand what the

words were saying but I liked the sounds they made,

Betty Botta bought some butta,
But the butta was too bitta,
If she put it in her batta,
It would make the batta bitta.
So,
Betty Botta borta
Betta bitta butta,
And she put it in her batta,
And the batta was NOT bitta,
So,
'Twas betta Betty Botta bought a betta bitta butta.

Real Sunday pudding was usually a bit more special. Like Queen's Pudding, with its fluffy white top and jewels of jam sitting on the soft yellow sponge underneath. It was just like the new Queen Elizabeth's crown. But puddings didn't have their own days like dinners and depended on what was in the garden or in the pantry. We had strawberries or raspberries in summer, then crumbles with plums, greengage and finally apple in the autumn. There were always milk puddings with rice or semolina (but Daddy wouldn't eat them because of something to do with the war). In the cold winter we would have Spotted Dick, or Treacle Pud in a basin tied up in a flat white hat. Jellies and trifles were just for Christmas and birthdays. Birthdays

were special because you had icing on top of your cake as well as in the middle. And it was pink.

It was Daddy who lit the front room fire on Sunday afternoons. I expect he thought he could do it better than Mummy. Mummy always rolled up sheets of newspaper and tied them in a knot, putting the pieces of coal on top then lighting the paper. Sometimes the paper all burnt away too fast and left the coal all black and then it was "a stupid old fire" and she had to roll up some more. If that didn't work she did a very scary thing and put a whole newspaper over the fireplace which made the flames roar up the chimney and nearly set light to the whole house. Daddy didn't use paper. Instead he got a little chopper and chopped up some of his leftover woodwork wood and the little yellow flames would dance and crackle around them until the little pieces of coal glowed bright and red. "What a lovely fire, look," Daddy would say proudly but Mummy never looked.

Daddy always got the Sunday tea too – it was sandwiches with Mock Crab. He mixed grated cheese with Heinz red sauce and Heinz salad cream and mashed it all to a paste with a fork. It tasted just like crab but without "that fishy taste" that Mummy didn't like.

For Sunday tea, the cakes, sandwiches and teacups went on the little gate-leg table in the front room and we were allowed to eat sitting on the armchairs – but not make crumbs, nor stand on your head because it made you sick.

Peabods and Bobble Gloves

I don't remember ever being cold in our house with its cosy coal fires and the podgy kitchen coke stove but sometimes parts of me did get quite cold outdoors. That was probably because I was much more concerned about rushing out to play than getting myself properly dressed. My very first snow made me cry – not because my feet were burning cold and purple in my socks-gone-to-sleep boots – but because I had to go BACK INDOORS! All the rubbing and warming in the world wasn't going to stop me crying because it wasn't my cold feet making me cry. I just wanted to go out and play in the snow again. Why didn't grown-ups ever know things like that?

The next time I went out in the snow, I got huge burning red blotches on my bare legs but I didn't cry for ages in case I got taken indoors again. When I did go in crying Mummy said they were "horrible chaps", even though I was sure I hadn't seen anyone else outside. Then she rubbed in some horrible thick, sticky cream which made it hurt even more. Why didn't Mummy know the cream did that?

After that, Daddy helped me get dressed properly. Getting dressed properly seemed to take an unbearably long time and I was afraid all the snow would melt before I got out there. First came the underwear with the little red ladybirds on which I just HAD to look at before they went on in case they were playing an interesting game. The itchy cream woollen vest had very annoying little cap sleeves which scrumpled up uncomfortably under your top clothes. But before your top clothes you had to put on your Pea-Bod. No-one else I asked had ever worn a Pea-Bod. (Some of them said they wore a Liberty Bodice but that didn't sound anything like as nice.) My Pea-Bod was a little bright white cotton waistcoat with tiny square white buttons and rows of stitches down the front making a stripy pattern. It was warm and cosy and hugged you tight but it did sometimes make the woolly vest underneath a bit more itchy. To finish off the fastenings there was a hook and eye that was scary because it looked like it might want to hook your finger. Then came my long beige woollen socks, which always made me think of chicken broth and get all hungry. Daddy did one sock and I had to watch and do the other but I couldn't scrunch it all up and put it straight on like he did. I took hold of the top rib and pulled and pulled until the poor stretched sock came right up over my knee. Then the little heel ball sat on top of my foot instead of underneath and I had to start all over again. Halfway there and time for a quick somersault on the bed!

Next half now.

Dresses had to be done by Daddy because they put the butttons AND the bow right round the back where I couldn't see to fasten them – why did they make them like that? It meant the big lumpy bow stuck in your back when you sat down to watch *Watch with Mother*. That was a really bad design fault. Next came the cardigan. Mummy was always knitting cardigans in spare 'mo-mens' but they were in horrid sensible colours, not the bright reds or yellows I would have liked and they always had far too many buttons. I think there must have been more buttons than holes because by the time I'd buttoned up to the top there were always one or two left with no holes to go into. Sometimes, instead of a dress, Daddy decided that I'd have to wear my warm corduroy trousers. Sometimes Daddy got this important decision horribly wrong. If I'd been in the middle of a cowboy game, trousers would have been just the right clothes. If I was playing "mummy" with my doll they were definitely the wrong ones and I refused to wear them in a kicking-and-screaming-and-rolling-over-the-bed way until I was the "naughty little girl who wasn't allowed out at all". You just HAD to wear the proper clothes for the game. Why didn't grown-ups ever know that sort of thing?

In the end, when he'd had a cup of tea, Daddy usually gave in. On top of all those warm clothes went my custard-yellow corduroy duffle-coat with the toggles that wouldn't wiggle through the woggles. And then my red gloves. Of all the clothes I had to wear, these seemed to me to be the most useless of all. First, they never had the right amount of holes for your fingers and you had to end up with two fingers sharing one hole. Then, they let the snow and wet straight through and when you touched the snow all the red colour came out and made the snow go pink. 'Worstest' of all, though, were the little pink icy bobbles which grew like tiny tennis balls all along your fingers and got so heavy that your gloves fell off and got lost in the snow. You might as well not put them on in the first place. Why didn't grown-ups ever know all these things?

Best Friends

There were no children living immediately 'nexdoor' to us so instead I was allowed to call on my grown-up friends. "Can you play today?" I'd ask and was always invited in, even if they were really busy.

Mrs Henry lived in the joined-on house 'nexdoor' where everything was the wrong way round and needed long investigation each time I went there to make sure it hadn't turned the proper way round like our house. I helped with the cooking, or sometimes we'd roll up balls of wool or play with buttons.

Once, she was very excited when I called and she told me to look in her front room. On the fireside rug was an enormous crêpe paper cracker as big as the whole rug but I didn't know what to do with it and stood there frozen in confusion until she said kindly, "Let's unwrap it together," and she slowly revealed from within the crackly paper a beautifully knitted yellow doll's dress – as big as a baby's so it would fit Big Susan my walking doll. My face twisted and froze in a contorted smiley way so I couldn't say thank you – or indeed anything at all – but she understood and told me to look inside the cracker again. The crackly paper unfolded to reveal a matching yellow overcoat with a ribboned bonnet, a pair of knickerbockers and finally two tiny little ribboned bootees. I have them to this day, despite them being worn constantly by Big Susan. Mummy said Mrs Henry had sneaked round secretly to measure my doll after I'd gone to bed. It wasn't a Birthday or Christmas present, just a Friendly sort of present which Mummy said was because she didn't have any babies of her own. I wondered why she didn't just go to the shops and buy a baby doll like mine to play with. Then we could both take out our doll's prams down the road together.

Mrs Lincoln lived across the road and I often went back with her to play after she'd been for coffee. She had a dresser in her kitchen which was magic because you opened the front and out slid a big white table, with all your cooking things on the shelves behind it. She was always making things with peeled apples which I wasn't allowed to do but I did mix the sponge and lick the bowl.

She had a funny thumb which was all purple and stiff – just like my hands went when I'd been out in the cold without gloves.

"Is your thumb cold?" I asked and she answered,

"Arthur Wright is."

I wondered for a long time who Arthur Wright was. I thought perhaps he might live outside in her garden.

Mrs Goodrun lived next door to her and was Mummy's best friend so we called her Auntie Mia. She was Welsh which meant when she went home on holiday there were mountains next to the sea instead of sand-dunes which was sad because that meant she couldn't make sand-castles. She had a Big Boy and when he went to Big School (where they wore very important blazers with a badge) she went to work in their fish-shop and then came home to get his tea before he cycled home again. Once when it was his birthday she came home early to get a special tea and I helped to make the cake that had blue icing instead of pink because he was a boy. When the Big Boy came home with his big friend, who also had a very important blazer with a badge, I was invited to stay for his tea-party. I had never been to a Big Boys' Party before and didn't know what to do at one, so I just stood in the corner while they played games. At tea-time we went into the dining room where three ducks were flying across the wall. I stood facing the wall and talked to the ducks while the boys ate and talked very loudly with their mouths full. Auntie Mia stayed in the kitchen – because they were Big Boys now – and wrapped up some cake specially for me to take home in a dark blue napkin.

"Mummy, can I have a Big Boys' Party?" I asked as I skipped home in the dark with Mummy. "At Big Boys' Parties you run fast round and round the settee and then slide down the back onto the cushions and kick them onto the floor!"

Mummy said, "Oh dear," in a worried sort of way but I thought Big Boys' parties looked really exciting.

When I got a bit older, I was allowed to walk right down to each end of the road – but never as far up as the main road or as far down as the scary deep hole that was once a clay-pit. That was how I met two more friends nearer my age. At the top end, in a tiny brick cottage down a narrow orchard path, lived Daniel. Daniel was a Medium Big Boy, not quite at Big School yet but in the Juniors. He was allowed to walk to school all on his own but he didn't go to school at all if it was raining. His mummy said he had trouble with his waterworks. Mummy and I often walked past the waterworks on our way to the shops. It was a tall red building with circle patterns on it made from blue bricks. At the top of the towers it had tall archways that should have been windows but they were filled in. I looked around Daniel's garden but I couldn't see any brick towers. He did have lots of giant square tins though, which he kept

caterpillars in and they kept escaping because he rather stupidly hadn't covered them with a lid. He gave me one hairy black caterpillar and I kept it in my red sea-side bucket. I put a paper lid on and Daddy pricked some little holes with a pencil tip so it could breathe and we gave it some "greens". One day it had gone and all that was left was a small bit of stick. I cried. Daddy just laughed and said it had turned into a 'crissliss' and when it woke up next spring it would turn into a pretty peacock. Mummy said she didn't want the bucket on her dresser for that long and certainly didn't want anything flying around the house so we put the 'crissliss' in a hole in a log down the garden. I kept going to look and see if it really had turned into a peacock – I thought it was pretty hard to believe, really. I never, ever, did see a peacock in the garden.

Daniel came round to play at my house sometimes but he always played with Daddy all the time and they got out the lawnmower and oil cans and not-very-interesting stuff. Mummy said it was nice for Daddy to have a little boy to play with sometimes so I used to go down to the bottom of the road to play with Tina, who always wore white but never got dirty.

Even though Tina was younger than me she already had a red metal pedal car that I jealously coveted. This car was allowed in the garden and we took turns driving down her long concrete path to the stream. She had other "nice" toys but some weren't allowed outside and she even had some which she wasn't supposed to play with at all. One of these was a huge wooden rocking horse and of course I rode on it and got into huge trouble with her granny. I had never, ever, been shouted at before and I asked if I could go home now please, not returning until the fierce grey granny had outstayed her two-week stay. Not learning my lesson from this episode, I then explored the forbidden giant dolls' house, rearranging the furniture into what I felt was a far more suitable arrangement. As this initially required gutting the little rooms first to obtain a suitable empty state for redecoration, I fell into trouble again. This time it was from Tina's daddy. I think I was quietly but sternly reprimanded but as he was Polish I couldn't understand him at all and I asked if I could go home again, please. Tina's third precious toy was a huge fully sprung dolls' pram and it was a horrid grey colour. Luckily I didn't like grey so it was left on display in its corner.

We kept to the garden after those little episodes. Tina was allowed outside with her white clothes on but she never got dirty like me. Once when I got dirty it was all because she made ME collect all the sticks. We needed them to build our scarecrow and the sticks were embedded in the black mud left after the storm when the tree fell down. We tied the sticks together for its arms, impaled a plastic ball on top for its head and crowned it with Tina's daddy's hat. (Please note that TINA fetched this.) Then we stuck it in the mud where the birds had been eating the cabbages and went to hide behind the garage. Here we hid and waited and waited for hours and hours to see if it would scare the birds away. Disappointingly, no birds came.

After a while, Tina's mummy came out to see why we were so 'spishoshly' quiet and I was in trouble yet again! She asked why had I taken Tina's daddy's hat and why was I covered in dirt and dust and cobwebs when Tina, who was wearing white, hadn't got the slightest bit dirty at all?
I just asked if I could go home now, please.

The Flood, The Fire and The Brimstone

My cosy, safe and happy childhood days were occasionally interrupted by disasters. Luckily these disasters managed to skirt harmlessly around our family but still came close enough to allow me a few adventures of my own with them.

One day the sky grew grey and menacing and a bright crackly light in the sky made Mummy hold her head tightly and run into the house, dragging me in by the hand. Once inside there was an enormous CRACK and RUMBLE that went on rumbling far away into the distance. Mummy didn't like it.

"Quick! Put all the knives away in the drawers!" she flapped and then we had to go and sit where it was safe in the middle of the house, which was luckily just where our settee was, so we read some books. Soon giant raindrops spat and thudded against the windows until it was all one big wetness and you couldn't see out and it was all quite fun really, except Mummy kept ducking down and screwing up her eyes when the bright light flashed – so perhaps I wasn't quite as safe as I felt. The rain went on raining hard all night and I could hear loud voices and screams out in the dark but Mummy came into my room and said, "Sleep tight," so I knew everything was all right.

In the morning we didn't have a road any more, we had a river. The brown river was lapping up against our front doorstep. It wasn't on the back lawn or the vegetables but the bottom of the garden was one huge lake with the little hawthorn trees poking their heads out of the swirling brown water. The rain had stopped by now and the sun came out and made a bright big rainbow over the white house in the distance where you could always hear Big Girls playing. I couldn't hear them playing at all that day. I wondered why.

Back out at the front it was getting really interesting because the Big Boy who lived opposite had got his blue-and-red canoe out and was paddling down the road. How I wanted a canoe like that. He paddled right down to the end of the road to talk to a man in another boat but this one was a yellow rubber one and people were putting bags of stuff into it through their windows.

After a day or two the water began to creep back away from our front garden and Daddy could just walk down the road in his rubber boots without it coming over the top but I couldn't get past nextdoors' gate before it came over mine. Daddy came home and told me I must NOT go down the road without holding his hand tightly because a Big Boy had just gone paddling down there and had paddled straight into the deep, deep clay-pit because the water was hiding the edge.

"Aaaa!" exclaimed Mummy and went very grey, "Has he been drowned?" and then it became frightening. Daddy said he was rescued by the yellow boat but HAD swallowed the filthy brown water and had to go to the hospital and have it all pumped out again. I didn't like the sound of that, imagining Daddy's bicycle pump down the boy's throat. Daddy went back out to help people rescue things from their houses but Mummy said people were far

more valuable than things, so she stayed to look after us and made coffee for The Lincolns whose goldfish had all swum out of their pond into the flood and were "probably swimming out to sea by now".

Tina, the little girl who lived down the road and always wore white but never got dirty, came to stay with us until her bungalow had dried out. Her mummy and daddy came too and slept in Mummy's bed and Mummy and Daddy slept downstairs on the 'put-you-up' which was the squeaky folded-out settee.

Gradually the floodwaters subsided a bit more and I persuaded Tina, who always wore white but never got dirty, that it would be safe now to go and play down the bottom of the garden, where a very naughty not-allowed visit had revealed a waist-high pool of water surrounding the big hawthorn tree. The mud had cleared from the water and the little shoots of grass swayed to and fro at the bottom. It was most inviting. Tina came along in her new red rubber boots so she wouldn't get dirty but I had only bare feet and underwear – which was all carefully pre-planned. When we got to the pool I withdrew my hidden bathing costume from under my vest and got changed into it, then much to Tina's horror I waded shoulder-deep into the bottle-green pool and waved my arms under the soft cool water.

"Come in," I said "it's lovely," but it wasn't lovely at all and I had to force a very false smile because beneath my feet and squashing up between my toes were all the fat, pink, dead worms which had drowned in the flood. I was really quite pleased when Tina's daddy came running down to rescue me to her cries of, "Quick! She'll drown!" even though I knew I was perfectly safe with my feet on the bottom with the fat, pink worms.

The real disaster was the fact that I was not allowed outside again until ALL the water had gone back to its home between the riverbanks. Then, accompanied by grown-ups, we were allowed to go fishing from it with our brand new fishing nets to catch the little silver minnows by the weir.

I feared fire much more than flood and was constantly in fear of our chimney catching fire like the one down the road, when giant yellow flames leapt out of the red chimney pot, trespassing where they weren't allowed to be and bringing a bell-clanging fire-engine with a ladder and shiny brass helmets down our bumpy road. The hoses looked just like fat black snakes and the firemen smelt sooty, like our fireplace.

It was mostly scary and only a little bit exciting.

The scary, sooty smell hung around the houses for days, so on the first really breezy day Mummy opened all the house windows wide and my pink sail-cloth curtains flapped and fluttered like a ship at sea. Tina was playing up in the bedroom with me and for some while I had been studying the window, walking along its inside length and measuring from one end to the other with my arm-span.

"Watch this." I said to Tina, who was wearing white but hadn't got dirty, and I climbed up onto the OUTSIDE sill of the left window. With an anxious gasp from my friend below I reached out past the closed middle bit and grabbed the solid frame of the far right open window. With a very firm hold with both hands and thus feeling perfectly safe, I began to walk along the OUTSIDE upstairs windowsill.

Unfortunately I was spotted from down below where Tina's mummy had been enjoying a cup of coffee with Mummy and Mrs Lincoln. Tina's mummy screamed and spilled her hot coffee all down her dress, then screamed again because it hurt. Mrs Lincoln told her to, "Be quiet, you silly thing!" and then calmly told me to keep very still and

Mummy would come up to help. I didn't think I needed any help, thank you.

"It's all right, I can reach right across and get back in through the other window. I've measured it," I replied confidently and sure enough I did and jumped safely back down onto the carpet next to Tina. I couldn't understand what all the fuss was about. Daddy had to be told when he got home, so that made it the FOURTH telling-off in one day and then everyone down our road got to hear about it and they ALL told me off too. I knew I could do it without falling. Why didn't grown-ups understand that?

After these little adventures there was much talk of "learning to do what you're told" and other threats to freedom such as "you won't be able to do that AT SCHOOL". Mummy said I was a good girl really but just needed to mix with others of my own age – before I WENT.

Tina was a good little girl all the time and never got dirty even though she wore white and Tina went to Sunday School. Tina's mummy said I should go too as it would make us both good and might help me prepare for real school.

So, just as the first signs of spring emerged and the yellow Brimstone butterfly danced freely through the spring-beams, I lost my carefree

Sundays. I had to put on horrid best clothes and walk sensibly along to the little tin hut with a curved roof next to the big church. We all sat in little circles around a Big Girl and she read stories to us and gave us sticky pictures of Jesus and Mary and all the saints to stick in a little yellow book. That wasn't so bad but when I'd heard all the stories I had to start going to Big Sunday School in the big church. I wasn't quite so well-behaved there because there weren't any cosy stories and I couldn't hear what the man at the front was saying. I didn't like his long black frock either. I began to get bored and fidgety and drop things under the pew in front where the man-at-the-front's wife sat. She kept going, "Sssh!" with a frown and spoke in whispers to Mummy afterwards. I stopped going to Sunday School soon after that. I didn't mind.

Another thing happened at the same time as the Brimstone butterfly appeared but it wasn't until years later that I learned exactly what. One evening Mr and Mrs Lincoln called round, which was a bit odd because it was evening and far too late for coffee. Then, strangely, they went upstairs with Mummy and Daddy and stared out of the front room window towards the cottages along the lane. I followed far enough behind so as not to be told to go away. There were bells ringing, just like our new telephone but far away on the main road and going towards the lane.

"Is it a fire?" gasped Mrs Lincoln and I imagined the fireman clanging the golden bell on the shiny red fire-engine.

"Is their chimney on fire?" Mummy asked and I prickled with fear and saw fat black hoses in my head.

"That's a police car I reckon," Mr Lincoln said gravely as another one clanged down the main road and I imagined the smartly polished black police car with its bell on the silver bumper. And then, much to my extreme annoyance, I was sent to bed right in the middle of the whole adventure because it was getting late and "everything will be all right again when it's morning".

I supposed everything was all right because Daddy lit the fire and we had breakfast as usual. I didn't ask why one neighbour after the other called in and chatted because it meant biscuits and orange juice EACH time someone came and I didn't want to interrupt the flow of food. I didn't understand what "A Murder at the Mill" meant anyway. It sounded like a rather dull board game.

"The old lady was found in her armchair," Tina's mummy whispered and I thought they were talking about Hide-and-Seek but then Mr Lincoln said, "Not caught yet," so I supposed that whatever had happened at The Mill, they hadn't caught any little silver minnows yet.

In the end, everyone stopped coming round and the biscuit tin got put away in the pantry. I was far more interested in playing outside with the yellow Brimstone butterflies than working that one out. Apparently no-one else has ever solved the murder mystery either.

An Apple for the Teacher

Towards the end of my blissful, secure and happy days, the word "school" began to casually crop up with increasing frequency. I supposed that was fine because "school" was the little place with the stone archway where the girls skipped out to meet their mummies wearing pale blue ribbon sewn around their little grey jackets with matching ribbons in their long dancing pigtails. I wouldn't have minded skipping through that little archway. What I did mind was being told that I must "always do what your teacher says," because I wasn't quite sure of what would happen if I didn't. I didn't want the teacher to send me to prison. (A policeman on a motorbike stopped our car once and told me off for throwing a lollipop stick out of the window. I was sure I'd be sent to prison then but Daddy said he was a clown, so perhaps I was just supposed to laugh at him.)

In our road there were very few children of my age, apart from Tina who was a year younger and "couldn't start yet". The only boys I knew were cousins in Norfolk and Daniel up the road, who preferred to play with Daddy when he came round anyway. I was happy playing with our grown-up neighbours helping them cook or garden. I wasn't really prepared for the free-for-all of lots of children. The thought of it all gave me a "nervous tummy", which is not really being ill at all "so you still have to go to school anyway".

When I did go to school I was taken to a nasty modern grey

building, with a round grey playground, down a long grey path. There was no old stone archway to skip under. Perhaps we were going down the back path for the bakers and milkmen.

I was given a seat next to Marcelle because she knew all about school as she had a brother in the Juniors. I sat in that seat all day long whilst the other children explored the water tray, played in the sandpit, pretended in the Wendy-house and painted on easels because no-one had told me I was allowed to move out of my seat. Next day the teacher told me to follow Marcelle around because she knew all about school as she had a brother in the Juniors. Marcelle and I soon found a cosy corner behind some tall folding bookcases full of exciting sets of books all colours of the rainbow. We eagerly read through the brightest coloured books – I could read fluently already and so could Marcelle because she had a brother in the Juniors – but when I picked up one particular book she shouted,

"No, we're not allowed to read that until we know the HARD WORD in it!"

"Where's the word?" I asked nervously.

She flicked nimbly through the pages until the scary hard word jumped out at us.

"AEROPLANE," we both chorused in horror.

"That's a REALLY hard word."

"I know. Because of the 'ae' bit."

"I'll never be able to read aeroplane," I said worriedly.

"You will, because we have to draw lots and lots of aeroplanes

and write 'aeroplane' underneath and when we can read the word without the picture underneath, Miss lets us read the book," Marcelle imparted knowledgeably. Well, that was all right then.

We left out that book and over the next few days we read through all the other books right up to the thick heavy ones called *High on a Hill* and *Far Away and Long Ago*.

"Now we have to ask to go and get books from the junior classes because we've finished all the infants' books," Marcelle said. Marcelle knew all about school because she had a brother in the Juniors. The Juniors seemed far too scary to visit even if her brother was there, so we painted on the easels after that. For the rest of that year we drew aeroplanes until we were allowed to start Book One.

Our head teacher was Miss Ping. She had a very round pale face and very short white hair, making it impossible for you to look at her without thinking of a ping-pong ball. This made talking to her a very hazardous affair due to the almost inevitable consequence of calling her Miss Ping-Pong by mistake . . . or worse still, Miss Pong. To be safe, I decided never to speak to her at all. For some reason, she didn't really like me much because of that.

I kept wondering when I would start skipping under the stone archway at the real school with the pretty blue-ribboned jackets. Miss Ping's school had a uniform but Miss Ping said no-one had to wear it. So it wasn't really a uniform at all.

Mummy had taken me to her favourite Ladybird shop to buy my school outfit and bought me a horrid brown pleated skirt. The pleats were uncomfortable to sit on and the straps crossed over on your back where you couldn't reach to cross them over. Then when you sat down the straps fell off your shoulders. It was horrid. A pretty powder-blue blouse was MEANT to be worn underneath but Mummy fell in love with an emerald green polka-dot poplin with puff sleeves, so I had to wear that instead. The poplin was crisp and cold and I hated the silly puff sleeves, which wouldn't fit under my cardigan. The cardigan was supposed to be pale blue but Mummy said that blue wasn't a nice colour for a girl and knitted me a sensible fawn one instead. Nobody else in my class wore that colour. Most children wore just parts of the uniform while their mummies saved up for the rest so we were a proper paint-box mix.

The only ones who wore ALL the uniform were The Twins. Mummy said it made them look so sweet but still wouldn't buy it all for me because I would grow out of it too fast. They wore pretty powder blue shirts and jumpers, brown ties with blue stripes, brown skirts and shorts and brown blazers with a beret and cap with the school badge on. I pleaded for a tie (because Daddy wore one) and a blazer with a badge but instead I was presented with a ghastly brown gabardine mackintosh that "you can wear when you're anywhere and will be big enough to fit until you are eleven," which, unfortunately, it did.

Marcelle, who knew all about school as she had a brother in the Juniors, wore a spotty turquoise pinafore dress with a pretty orange jumper. And red shoes.

How I wished I could have red shoes.

We ALWAYS had to buy our shoes in the Clark's basement department where "they know how to fit them properly". You had to climb up and stick your feet in a green X-ray machine which could see the bones in your feet right through your new shoes. I did like going there though because they always had huge moving models of fairytales – sometimes The Seven Dwarves hammered away at their jewel-mine or sometimes The Mad Hatter stuffed The Dormouse into a teapot. We were allowed to stand and watch them whilst Mummy bought uninteresting things like towels from another department in the store. I think the shop was called 'Boms'. The other fun thing in 'Boms' was that when you paid for your things the money was placed in a brass tin hanging from an overhead wire which whizzed off somewhere like the electric train on the London line. Best of all about 'Boms' though, was that Father Christmas went there BEFORE Christmas and you could go and tell him exactly what you wanted.

Anyway, back to the shoes. I was always bought the same kind of shoes 'cept' one size bigger each time – a brown brogue for winter and brown sandals with a cream crêpe sole and little cut-out leaves on the toe for summer. I wasn't in dispute about the pattern. It was the colour. I wanted red. I wanted red so much that I was actually brave enough to say so to the selling lady and to say so right up to a full-blown tantrum until the shop manager appeared and said in a deep stern voice that "We don't have that colour available in your size, madam."

And then we left with the brown ones. I knew he was telling a Huge Big Fib because the lady had just let me try the red ones on – just for a little while, as a special treat.

We were sometimes allowed special treats at school but it usually meant something nasty would follow. Once, Miss Ping opened a Tuck Shop in her office. For 1d you could buy a fat hard lollipop which was so big you couldn't finish it in one playtime and had to throw it in the bin. The apples were 1d too but they had a hard skin and no-one was there to peel them so they went in the bin as well. Miss Ping always tried to make us buy Potato Puffs

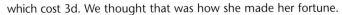

which cost 3d. We thought that was how she made her fortune.

Once, in 'Sembly', she started to talk about the Tuck Shop and about a terrible thing she had seen. I began to get a little bit hot because that very morning I had bought a lollipop even though I knew it was bad for my teeth and she had asked me if I was SURE that's what I wanted. SHE MUST BE ABOUT TO TALK ABOUT ME IN FRONT OF THE WHOLE SCHOOL!

I began to grow hotter and hotter until my cheeks glowed red as a beetroot and I began shuffling and shook nervously. As Miss Ping spoke a dark grey cloud sank over the room. I could barely hear her words as she said, "Today I saw a little girl do a very foolish thing," and my head throbbed and pounded unbearably. "This girl had 3d and she COULD have bought some Potato Puffs – which are very good for you – but do you know what she did?" (and at this point I thought I would die), "She bought THREE apples . . . That would give her a very nasty tummy-ache wouldn't it? It's far, far better to buy Potato Puffs instead."
How I sighed with relief.

I don't remember learning much at school. I thought the counting blocks were for building houses with and the strings of beads for making pull-along trains. We often played with water which is always fun, even if we weren't allowed to mix in a little soil and make a delicious brown sludge. There was a huge metal water tray with four metal jugs that we had to fill – a giant gallon, smaller quart and pint and the tiniest, cutest little gill. It took us 33 gill-fulls to fill the giant gallon but I think some got a bit spilt. It got spilt when a naughty boy pushed past us to the drinking fountain, a little bubbly stream turned on by a sideways tap which flowed upwards into your mouth then ran down into a little saucer with drain-holes. This boy slurped up two whole 'cheekfuls' then spat the whole lot out into the fountain. First our teacher went very, very red. Then, getting really, really close up to the boy, she suddenly exploded with little bits of white spit, spotting on his face.

"Now ALL the water pipes will have to be turned off," she screamed "and you'll have to be flushed and sterilised!"

At that point I made the decision to have nothing to do with that teacher in future, in case she decided I might have to be flushed and sterilised too. That's why to this very day, I still don't know if that dear little jug is called Jill or Gill because I was too scared to ask her.

That poor school. It tried very hard with me but its only lasting legacy was the ghastly brown gabardine mackintosh with its tightly buckled belt and its silly, floppy brown hood. That followed me all the way through my next school – where the uniform was blue.

SEVEN
IN THE
SIXTIES

Going Out West

Daddy had a Promotion. I didn't know what that was but it sounded like a very bad pain. I had an operation once because of a bad pain in my ear. The Promotion was bad enough for us all to drive home to Norfolk to discuss it with the family. On arrival there were initially lots of "Ooo!'s" and "Ahhs" and "Well dones!" until Daddy said it was NOT a Promotion back to Head Office but a job, "... in the west." Wow!

The West was where Cowboys and Indians were. Well at least nobody was going to have an operation, so I breathed again and listened from my hidey-hole under the huge kitchen table, stroking the sleeping dog.

All our family had lived in Norfolk for ever and ever. They thought there was no other place TO live. Although we now lived in a neighbouring county, it was still just about alright. It was still East Anglia and we would soon be back, or so they thought.

"So, so far away," Granny sighed.

"There's inntstree out there," scorned an uncle,

"Nasty, dirty ole stuff," another added.

"Yar woont like it oova thare," Great Uncle Horace chirped cheerily from his wing chair.

"But I'll get a new car and much more salary," Daddy broke in. I hated celery.

Then the only other relation who had ever lived outside Norfolk interrupted, "You can be happy wherever you live. You don't HAVE to live in Norfolk. It's NOT the most important place in the world." The family fell into stunned and baffled silence. I too was shocked.

Were you even ALLOWED to say that?

Well, we did decide to move out west to where the 'inntstree' was, although I still wasn't quite sure what 'inntstree' was, apart from it being brown and dirty. It sounded a bit like mud pies and I liked making them so I wasn't too bothered.

It was a very long journey so we drove overnight and my little sister and I slept on mountains of bedding on top of suitcases and boxes, with the back seat of the car folded down. It was our brand new Morris Minor which had "come with the Promotion". I hadn't seen The Promotion yet though, only the car.

Waking up, I glared sleepily out of its rear window at the rising sun just as we drove over a cream-coloured bridge spanning a swirling brown river. It was not at all like the slow bottle-green rivers of home – perhaps THAT was what 'inntstree' was. Not too bad then. I yawned and looked out to the front.

"Mountains!" I exclaimed, nudging my sister awake as some enormous dark green hills loomed up ahead of us.

"What's all those little white boxes on them?" she asked with one eye open.

"Houses." replied Mummy rather less impressed. "Perhaps one of them will be ours. I hope the hills aren't too steep or we'll fall over the edge," she said worriedly. She had only lived in flat places before now.

Above the little white boxes on the golden, grassy slopes, herds of tiny little white animals were moving and I could just make out two horseback riders. That must be the cowboys rounding up their cattle, I thought. I wished I was one of those cowboys.

The Home in the Hills

While we looked for a new house we stayed in a huge pink granite stone house in the clouds, up high in the hills. It was called *Wychcrest* and was once a boarding school. After it closed, the lady who owned it decided to let lots of people stay with her there, probably because of all the spare beds she had left over.

Two other families were staying there too while they looked for new houses. Luckily all the children got on, because we all knew how to ride pretend horses and happily rode all day long in the huge rambling overgrown gardens. There were only two places we weren't allowed to play in and these were barred by red painted gates. When we went through the first red gate we found ourselves in a massive vegetable garden which didn't interest us much – but the shed did. We could see that a witch lived there because there was a broomstick leaning against it and when we touched it a voice shouted, "Oi!" in a low voice that was obviously the witch trying to pretend she was only the gardener.

We scarpered back through the red painted gate and left the witch alone after that.

"I know why your house is called *Witch Crest*," said one of the younger boys to the landlady and his bigger brother quickly trying to change the subject foolishly added,

"Your vegetable garden is looking very good!"
The landlady just smiled back with a little tiny twitch in the corner of her mouth.

The landlady lived with us all in the big house, but she was a little disorganised about having people to stay so all our rooms were scattered higgledy-piggledy all over the house. Our rooms were above another family's kitchen whilst their rooms were above our kitchen. The second family had the large downstairs rooms and their tiny kitchen was upstairs next to our rooms. Daddy tried to point out this awkward living arrangement to the landlady but she got flustered and had a bad 'Ass-mar' attack and kept gasping, "Ass...ass...ass-mar..."
The littlest boy giggled and got sent to bed even though he wasn't laughing at the landlady, just at the rude word 'ASS-mar'. Why didn't grown-ups ever understand?

"How old are you?" I asked her grey face, as she sat recovering in her chair.

"Ninety-nine," she smiled and then I felt sorry for her because that meant she would probably only live one more year. Nobody gets to be more than A Hundred. To make up for it, every morning just before eight o'clock, I ran down the long drive and opened the gate for her, as she drove the 30-mile trip to her new teaching job.

I wanted to live in that big old house forever, where there were grassy hills to hurtle down, tall trees to climb, hedges to hide in and thickets for thorny dens. However, our new house was finished and Mummy said we'd never be cold any more so down, down, down into town we went.

Estate

We had taken a long while to choose our house on the new estate even though only a few had actually been built by then. Daddy had always wanted to build his own "split-level" house, so we first went enthusiastically to view one of those. Daddy had really wanted to be a builder but Granny wanted him to wear a suit. That house though didn't suit Mummy.

"Ohh! The front door opens straight into the dining room!" Mummy exclaimed and said it would be "too draughty".

"And the sitting room is down there!" she flustered. It was down a long flight of stairs which would be "dangerous". To add insult to injury, the smallest bedroom (to be my sister's) was downstairs by the sitting room.

"She might cry herself to death in the night and never be heard!"

It was out of earshot from the main bedrooms that were up a second staircase, off the dining room.

Mummy clearly didn't like "split-levels". Daddy and I did. I especially liked the huge gardens that ran down to a long row of tall willows by a bubbling stream. But it was "not a proper house" to Mummy's mind. She found a row of proper houses with a proper upstairs and downstairs and a proper hall and landing, overlooking the huge school playing fields and the hills beyond so we had a "room with a view".

She still wasn't quite sure which was the most proper of these houses and surprisingly chose one with its front door at the side – which I thought wasn't at all proper. And it still wasn't quite right because it had a "through lounge".

"I wish it had a proper dining-room," she said and immediately I knew she was thinking about fish.

"You might get fish smells creeping all over the house," she said screwing up her nose.

The kitchens of these houses were very different to our old kitchen. Instead of cold, red quarry-tiles which you polished with red stuff from a flat round tin, the floor was covered with red linoleum which you could just wipe clean. There were white cupboards with long plain metal handles hanging from all the walls and, underneath those, a red formica worktop covering the whole length of the cupboards that stood on the floor – and they all fitted together with no gaps. The sink and drainer was all one stainless steel unit, not like our old huge white 'porslin' sink and wooden draining board and instead of "hot" and "cold" written on the taps there was a red and a blue blob instead. Perhaps the makers couldn't read. Mummy said she loved this really modern kitchen. What she didn't like was that we had no pantry. Instead there was one small tall cupboard in the corner, which Daddy said they put there because it wouldn't fit into the fitted kitchen. Which meant it wasn't a proper fitted kitchen like the one the builder had described.

What a job all this house-buying was. Daddy and I were happy with the first one.

As this house didn't have a nice cool pantry, we would have to buy a fridge to keep all the milk, butter and lard in. Mummy didn't like that

idea because "the butter won't spread, the lard won't crumble, the milk will make your tea too cold and the eggs won't cook properly".

Opposite the fridge space was a kitchen stove but not like our friendly old pot-bellied one which stood on bendy legs and looked like Aunty Vi. This one was white and square with a straight black chimney pipe. It did the same thing though, just not in such a friendly way, heating our kitchen and the hot water too. It had to burn oval-shaped anthracite balls of smokeless coal, not the dusty, smelly stuff our old boiler used. Daddy said there was a "Mershun heater" too, but it was "SPENSIVE" and only to be used in emergencies like if the boiler wouldn't "draw" when the north wind blew. Or in summer.

All the new houses were built for coal heating, each with a coal boiler but only one fireplace, so not as good as our old house which had a fireplace in all the big rooms including upstairs. Here, we would have to burn smokeless fuel which didn't make the tall pretty yellow flames that our old fireplaces had. None of these new houses had been built with any central heating, double-glazing or insulation and they were colder than our old house, with gaps round the windows and skirting boards and spaces between the floorboards you could lose your pocket-money down. Daddy said the builders had been in too much of a hurry and he could have done a far better job himself if he'd been allowed to be a builder. I didn't mind the cold too much because Jack Frost would often come and draw beautiful master-pieces on our bedroom windows, which you could scratch your own little patterns in with your fingernails.

The estate had been designed around the features of the old farm

it stole its land from. In the huge shady garden of the remaining old farmhouse, two old ladies would sit, blanketed in their cane chairs, and take Afternoon Tea under the huge cedar tree. They seemed completely oblivious to the chaos of mud, noise and building going around them and chatted and chinked quite happily in their own disappearing world. Their house was three floors high with long downstairs windows and littler ones as you went upwards. Its kitchen stuck out at the back and stables stuck out at the sides and although I wasn't tall enough to see if there were ponies inside, I just knew there must be. Of all the houses on our estate, I would have chosen to live in that lovely old farmhouse.

Our group of houses was built in the orchard and every house had been generously left at least one old apple or pear tree in their garden. Between us and the "split-levels" stood The Dingle, an old spinney with ancient stately elm trees, a tree that sadly only our generation can have the privilege of remembering. I would drift off to sleep at night watching the stars of The Plough dipping into the W-shape of the elm tree tops and listening to the owls haunting their hairy boughs.

The elms ran down to a wide strip of meadow left beside the cool willowed stream, smelling of ramsons and speckled with celandine, where a footpath ran through tall grasses onto The Common. It was a wonderland for us young children to play in – to build tree-houses in the willow boughs, make clay dams in the streams and make little dens and camp-fires in the thickets. Sadly all these little breathing spaces on the estate have now been felled and flattened for "in-fill" housing. Even The Common seems to have lost some of its wild nature with over-enthusiastic taming. Where do the children play now?

The final completion of our estate took another three years whilst diesely bulldozers sloshed through boot-high red mud and houses slowly encroached on the emerald green meadows that stretched right up to the railway line. Here we would lie in wait for the steam engines which loomed like roaring, hissing monsters from our lairs in the cool grass. When the last-ever bungalow was built

and a pretty ginger-haired girl moved in, we had to relocate our train-spotting to the red-brick railway bridge on The Common and lay on the parapet as the sulphurous steam engulfed us. It never dawned on us that it might be a little dangerous.

As the houses were finished the population of young families and children grew fast and it became a fashionable place to live for the new Sixties pop-art generation. Fitted carpets were bought to accompany the fitted kitchens and square teak furniture fitted tightly together along living room walls. New record-players sang with Sixties songs, cocktail parties coaxed out short shift dresses that no-one could move in and ladies wore strange white-coloured hair that stood up like beehives on top of their mascara-ed spidery eyelashes. I dreaded having to grow up and be like them, dress in tight mini-skirts and

decorate my house with shiny plastic furniture and garish circle-patterned wallpaper. I was probably not a Child of the Sixties! I liked our old things much better.

My parents had married at the end of the 1940s when the austerity of the war years still lingered on. They bought one set of oak furniture for their dining room with an oak Welsh dresser but the rest had to be family hand-me-downs or army surplus cupboards and drawers which Daddy stripped and painted. He made all our small stools, coffee tables and bookcases himself, making a "Saturday" smell with the raw wood and shavings. That old furniture outlived all the modern Sixties teak and and plastic and still lives with us today.

Daddy had made friends with the builders who brought him all the leftover timber, broken bricks and clay piping that they would otherwise have burned or buried. Daddy first made some tall trellis-work gates from discarded packing wood and painted them with a three-quarters-full tin of leftover white paint. Then he made all our garden paths by using unusable bricks, turning them over to hide the chips. For the patio, the builders gave him some leftover cement and old red quarry-tiles from one of the demolished farm outbuildings. He made the ground drains with leftover chipped pipes and reject drain covers. Behind the garage he laid concrete for the coal bunkers and a retaining wall with little round discarded drainpipes in to hold the garden up. Then, one day, Brian the bulldozer driver brought us a whole load of topsoil that one man said was "mud and he didn't want it in his back garden". So we had it instead and we made our lawn on top of it by rolling out long pieces of meadow-grass turf that they cut off before they dug new foundations. I knew Daddy loved this kind of work because he whistled. He knew how to do all these sorts of things properly, not like the builders did. It was a pity his mummy wanted him to wear a suit because he would have been a very good builder. He said he could have built six houses AND landscaped the gardens with all the leftover stuff they'd wasted on our estate. He even built us a little playhouse from the leftovers that weren't quite good enough for proper things – and a hutch for the rabbit.

I bet not many people know that recycling was invented by my daddy.

Two Wheels or Four

Most of the mummies on our estate didn't go out to work but worked in the house instead and looked after their children until they were big and left school. They didn't need a car. Some of the daddies could walk or cycle to work in the shops or the small nearby factories so they didn't need a car either. The people who did have cars had to work outside the town in places where the buses didn't go. Daddy was one of these and his office gave him a brand new car every three years because he had to drive out a long way to see his 'Surance Clients'. We were very lucky because they let him drive us in it even when he wasn't working so we were able to go out exploring the countryside in our succession of little grey Morris Minors.

Our 'Nexdoor Neighbours' had never had a car until they got a baby and thought they might need one if it got sick and they needed to drive it to hospital. They had lived in this town all their lives and had never been anywhere that buses didn't go to, not even venturing up into the hills that had watched over them all their lives. Eventually they bought a second-hand blue Triumph Herald with a pale blue stripe between the shiny chrome bits. Daddy tried to teach the man to drive but said he'd never learn because he was too scared of the car. He was even scared of it when it stood parked on the drive and placed huge blocks of wood under its wheels in case it "ran away" during

the night. It stood there until the baby was five years old. Then he HAD to drive it because he got a job further away and driving it was not so scary as moving house. They still live in the same house now.

Mummy learnt to drive once. Then Daddy announced that she wasn't going to drive any more. I thought that might have been because once she'd forgotten to stop and drove right through the wooden wall of our garage. Daddy built a brick one after that.

As the Sixties drew on, more and more ladies (apart from Mummy) were learning to drive and their car of choice was often the new Mini Minor. Daddy said that ladies liked them because they were much easier to drive (which made Mummy say "Poof!") and because they liked the bright new colours. Daddy said it "wasn't the sort of car a man should drive and the bright colours were totally unsuitable for business". We knew that when he said that sort of thing it was really because he wanted one himself. Two men at Daddy's hockey club, who didn't have wives, shared a bright red shiny MG sports car. It only had two tiny doors and no roof so it was a good job they didn't have wives or they might not have liked it. In the old days Daddy had a bright red sports car too but he had to get a sensible car with four seats when he married Mummy.

Daddy knew all about cars. Once one of his elderly lady clients asked him to look under her bonnet because her engine kept spluttering and coughing out blue smoke. When she took him out for a drive in it, Daddy told her it was probably better to find another place to hang her handbag from, instead of pulling out the choke and hanging it on there. He knew ALL about cars.

It seemed to me a 'both-ways' kind of time when half the people wanted to be new and modern and the other half wanted to stay in the sensible grey-and-black time. My uncle was a sensible sort. He proudly drove all the way from Norfolk to visit us once in his black Ford Prefect. He wasn't married then so his dog sat in the red passenger seat next to him. It used to make a strange kind of hissing noise (the car, not the dog) and you had to warm it up with the choke before it went anywhere (again, the car, not the dog).

If you were really, really rich you could have a bright shiny big car with four whole doors or one with sliding doors and an extra bit of roof so you could sleep in it and a big VW on the front. My headteacher bought a new green one when the school got two more classes and he went on a HUGE expedition and drove it all the way to France. It took him all the six weeks of the summer holiday and we had to keep hearing all about it afterwards in assembly. Every day. For nearly a year.

No Dedicated Follower of Fashion

It was a scorching hot dry day and we were ready for our summer holiday. We had been sent out to play in the garden in our old underwear as everything was washed, packed and ready for the long drive in the cooler evening. Suddenly out in the road a boy on a bike whizzed past screaming, "Fire on The Common, fire on The Common!" and he was rapidly joined by a posse of other screaming boys on bikes. I couldn't miss this – but not in my underwear – so I tore upstairs and found a

pair of my mother's old slacks. The waist was a bit big so I borrowed Daddy's braces and tore back down to the garage to get my bike.
Flat tyre!
Have to borrow Mummy's bike.

I couldn't reach the saddle but found I could pedal standing up and just about reach the handlebars. The long legs of Mummy's slacks however proved a problem, catching in the chain.
Panic! Can't miss a fire on The Common!
I found the answer in a pair of Daddy's green-and-white woollen hockey socks which I pulled over the slacks fixing the trouser-bottoms in place and securing the oversized sock feet in a pair of Mummy's pink "slip-on" shoes.

I arrived at The Common just as the fire had reached its spectacular height and just before the clanging fire engines arrived. Orange and red flames were licking the dry tree trunks and devouring the golden grass, with thick yellow smoke billowing up over the watching crowd. What I couldn't quite understand though, was why all the faces in the crowd were looking at me and not at the fire.

Friends and Relations

Following my fashion faux pas, I found it a little hard to make friends at first on our new estate. This was further compounded by initial misunderstandings of the new dialect which I mistakenly giggled at to begin with…I thought they were teasing with funny voices, saying "garse" for gas and "hart" instead of "hat". They also took rather longer to say things compared to our brisker eastern accent and I mistook it for disinterest in me. I decided to explore further afield in search of friends and wandered off the estate towards Pickersleigh. I hadn't gone far when I noticed a potential "climbing tree", an old oak high on a red clay cutting overhanging the path beneath. I scrambled up the bank and stood on the wide roots of the huge hollow tree assessing the best route of ascent.

"Can't climb that, it's The Gurral's Den!" a boy's voice spoke from the long grass. I jumped back in horror. I'd never heard of a Gurral and wondered what sort of an animal it was – maybe a bear. I knew bears lived out west. I ran home.

I returned a few days later, having been reassured that no bears or monsters could possibly live in an English oak tree, to find the boy from the long grass right up IN the tree. Seeing me watching – and being a boy – he edged his way along the branch overhanging the road and deftly swung down under the branch, dangling like a monkey.

"Can you drop?" I dared.

"Yeah. 'Course," he replied after a thoughtful pause and screwing

his eyes up tight he counted to three and landed painfully on the pathway down beside me.

"I thought you said it was a Gurral's den, "I challenged, allowing him time to turn away grimacing and smear a small tear down his cheek.

"'Tis. We share it. S'mine on Saturdays when The Gurrals go out." I wondered how an animal could know what day of the week it was, but made a note that it would be safe to climb the tree on a Saturday when it went out.

"Do you want to see The Gurrals, they'll be back soon?" the boy asked. I declined the offer but lingered with curious apprehension in the long grass on the bank, allowing for a quick getaway, as the boy sauntered off across the green to a long house. After a short while a nice smiley lady emerged from the house and made her way straight to my perfectly hidden hideaway.

"Hello," she smiled, "I wondered if you would like to come and play with my Gurrals?" and held out such a friendly hand that I bravely took it out of sheer curiosity. Indoors I was introduced, over squash and biscuits – to her two little GIRLS.

I soon became friends with the two little Gurrals and went over to play regularly. Their garden was long and rambling with plenty of room to play properly and keep interesting animals in wire runs. Once their uncles, aunts and cousins came to stay and brought some baby rabbits.

I sat down on a grassy knoll to watch the others being scratched by them.

"Don't sit there, the aunts will get you!" one of the girls squealed at me.

"What will they do?" I worriedly enquired and the girl lifted her skirt to reveal a huge swollen red mark on her leg.

"THEY BITE! Don't you know even that?" she laughed.

I didn't think it a laughing matter at all. My aunts would never do that. After that I didn't call on the girls for a while, hoping that their nasty relations would soon go home.

Instead, I made friends with a new boy in my class who also liked rabbits but wasn't allowed to have one.

"Why aren't you allowed?" I asked incredulously.

"'Cos I'm living with my aunt until we get our new house and she hates pets."

Now I understood.

"Oh. Aunts aren't very nice sometimes are they? Does she bite?" The boy paused and looked curiously at me, replying,

". . . Does yours?"

"No. But I know one that does."

The urge to keep rabbits remained with us despite the danger of aunts and we had come up with a plan. It required me to sneak secretly around to his aunt's house with a roll of wire netting, tapping it gently against his window, receiving the thumbs-up and then sneaking away. I then had to sneak back again because I'd forgotten that I was helping him dig the hole that the rabbit was to live in. We knew rabbits lived in holes. The wire netting was to go on top of the hole to keep the rabbit inside – and to hide the hole from the aunt we put grass over the top. We bought the rabbit for five shillings from a farm boy, who had lots of money in his piggy bank. Next morning though, the hole was bigger than the wire cover and the grass had all gone, along with the rabbit. The aunt must have found it. I felt sorry for children who had such nasty aunts.

I went home and counted the last bit of money in my own piggy-bank and bought the two remaining baby rabbits off the smiling farm boy, telling my new friend he could keep his at my house.

Parents sometimes react strangely to their children's good intentions though and there was a bit of a fuss about having to make TWO hutches and having to buy extra pet-food for someone ELSE'S pet. Even more confusing, when they didn't even want two rabbits, they said they'd have to buy yet another one for my little sister, to "make it fair". I didn't always understand parents.

"Actually that isn't really fair," I argued, "because I was seven before I was allowed one and she's having one when she's only three."

In the end she got a baby guinea-pig, because our rabbits scratched. My friend's scratching rabbit was returned but the farm boy said he hadn't enough money to give us our 5/- back. The guinea-pig had the rabbit's hutch and Daddy bought a "family dog" which you could stroke without being scratched. Our little family had grown rapidly from four to seven.

This was probably not the right time to push for a pony.

After a couple of weeks, calculating that the girls' aunts must have gone home by then, I went back to visit their baby rabbits and sat down again on the grassy knoll to watch them.

"Watch out! I told you before not to sit on there – look!" and the girls pointed to a mass of tiny red ANTS crawling all over the little knoll.

"They bite you know, look at my leg!"

Saturday is Shopping Day

The shops up town were on a very, very steep road. Mummy was afraid of steep hills because there weren't any where she came from. When you parked your car here you had to turn the front wheels towards the pavement so that if the brakes broke the car ran into pedestrians, or broke the shop windows, instead of running into the cars on the road. I thought they'd probably got that rule the wrong way round.

Most of the shops sold one kind of thing each, so there was a butcher, a bakery and cake shop; a shop that sold materials for dressmaking; shops for ladies' clothes, men's clothes and children's clothes as well as a stationers, bookshop, greengrocers, toy shop, china shop, Elts the shoe shop and so on. At the bottom of the shopping hill there was a small bare-wooden-floored 'Woolwuffs', selling pocket-money sweets and red plastic cowboys, and a small department store called 'Kenduls' where we bought our new beds. Up along the very top of this road, making a "T", were the posher shops that we only shopped in occasionally for school uniform or Daddy's new suit, although the ink-and-leather smelling W. H. Smith received our occasional custom when aunts sent us Book Tokens. The Banks were up here too. Banks were very serious and important places for "business", full of dark colours and smelling of polished wood. You had to be very good and keep very quiet – so I didn't like going in there at all.

It used to take us nearly all of Saturday morning to do our shopping, visiting the bank before all these little shops and having polite chats to the shopkeepers. Then a new kind of shop appeared which sold all different kinds of things in one big room and you could even buy your washing powder and soap there too. Mummy said that would make your bread taste soapy so we didn't try that for a long time. When we did, we had to take THEIR shopping basket and take things off the shelf without asking them politely and Mummy said it felt as though we were stealing – which was a big worry to me and I kept glancing round for a policeman. Then we took all our shopping to a lady in

red sitting by the door who you didn't have to speak to at all and then you had to put all the stuff into your own shopping basket and give them theirs back. Mummy didn't think that it was a very friendly way to shop so we didn't go there much.

I always held on tightly to Mummy's hand because the people shopping in this town seemed a little strange to me, not at all like the ones in our friendly Corner Shop. One man (who didn't use the new kind of shop either) carried all his shopping in a huge square basket on his head so his hands could hold onto all the strings that his children were tied to. His clothes were always very brightly coloured so I quite liked him but I wasn't too sure about the young men who wore black cowboy hats and purple scarves and spoke about the 'Thee-a-tarr' all the time. Daddy said they were a little "different" because some very clever and very "arty" people lived in that town. I wondered which was which and concluded that tying your children to your waist was quite clever because their mummy would have been quite cross if he'd lost them out shopping.

When we'd finished shopping we would go "for coffee" up some steep stairs to a place with a parrot. I had milk. My sister had squash but she never drank it all up. The parrot used to politely say, "Hello" every time someone came up the stairs but one day it started making very loud rasping, coughing noises like the old man who always sat on his own by the window. Then the parrot spat noisily and said a VERY rude word.

After that, the parrot wasn't allowed in the coffee-shop any more.

Toys and Toyshops

For some reason Mummy and Daddy always tried to avoid going past the toyshops. Toys were changing from metal to plastic. Plastic meant cheaper toys and there were lots more of them now. There were still good quality metal toys being made like the tiny Matchbox cars and the slightly bigger Dinky Toy cars but more accurate models for train-sets – which were MY interest – could now be moulded from plastic. I already had an O-gauge clockwork train-set, handed down from Daddy when his daddy died and the loft was cleared out – so it must have been very old. There was a red "Duke of York" engine, a black LNER goods engine, a little green Great Western shunter and a black real steam shunter that you lit with meths but were only allowed to watch Daddy do, in case the boiler burst. That made it scary so I didn't like that one. There were two Pullman passenger carriages with tiny chairs and tables inside and some goods and cattle trucks. The animals in the cattle trucks were made of metal and Daddy had played with them so much he had worn big holes in the side and rubbed the paint off until they were shiny. My own farm animals were clean and plastic and lived in a painted wooden farmyard but the tractors were the same old-smelling metal as the grey rails in Daddy's train-set.

A lot of the boys in my school had electric Triang train-sets. At first, I couldn't persuade my parents to buy me another train-set. Mummy said she didn't want me to play with boys' toys but I could see Daddy would

have quite liked to have one so persisted with the pleas until we got a real scale model OO set and laid it out on two huge boards in the garage. I spent the subsequent years meticulously modelling Airfix stations, signal boxes, bridges and engine-sheds whilst Daddy manufactured little model houses out of his collection of leftover builders' bits. We stuck them securely on to the board growing our own little model world.

The toyshop that sold the Airfix kits was owned by a Big Boy on our estate. He could have anything he wanted from his shop so his model railway occupied a whole room in his house and came completely ready-made. It even had working electric lights operated by a switch-board on the wall which only he was allowed to play with – even at birthday parties when you're 'sposed' to share.
We were impressed.

Daddy made me a huge sailing boat out of leftover builders' plywood and Mummy sewed the sails out of my old pink sail-cloth curtains, of windowsill-expedition fame. The yacht took a long time to make and even then we had to wait for the wood to 'stretch' in the bath, then the paint to harden before we took it to the pond on The Common to try it. The Big Boy from the toyshop saw us there and went home to fetch his boats too. He returned with two three-foot-long varnished

cruisers with real engines which he proceeded to steer across the pond right into our path. Being wholly dependent upon the wind direction we were unable to avoid him and spent the next few weeks repairing and adding poly-styrene buoyancy aids to our indignant yacht. We took it to a far-away pond on another common after that and had great fun with it. It still sits in my bathroom today. I think we had far more fun from our home-made toys than that Big Boy ever got from his shop toys but Mummy said we were not to be too harsh on him because both his parents worked six days a week and he was an "only child". This meant he was probably lonely and had lots of toys to make up for it. I wondered if I should try being lonely.

The Big Boy's toyshop also sold big expensive dolls but he didn't have any of those himself. When we bought dolls they were much cheaper and usually from 'Woolwuffs'. They were quite acceptable to us at first but this was the beginning of the big consumer age and even small children were becoming victims of the "latest trend". The "latest trend" and "must have" amongst my little sister's friends was the Barbie Doll and during the weeks up to Christmas she quietly dropped little hints. For some reason though, Mummy completely disapproved of poor Barbie and persuaded her to have Sindy instead, "because Sindy was a much nicer girl".

Luckily a few other mothers were also of this incomprehensible persuasion and so we set an alternative trend. Sindy arrived at Christmas to be followed on subsequent birthdays and Christmases by Sindy's red car, Sindy's boyfriend Paul and Sindy's little sister Patch.

Although the hardware had been approved of, the vastly overpriced sets of clothing were not, so these were painstakingly copied using leftover sewing scraps, skilfully created on Mummy's Singer sewing machine. Hence, we learnt to design, cut, sew, button and zip in the best way possible by some hilarious trials and errors and lots of fun. I kitted out a whole teddy bear football team once from old cotton pillowcases for shorts, Mummy's old blue dress for shirts, tiny knitted socks from wool remnants and football boots from old rubber boots. It meant I had a head start when it came to using the school's Singer machines, although my sewing teacher clearly disagreed on that point.

When I got a bit older and had 2/- a week pocket money I was able to buy my own things but it took a lot of saving up. First I started collecting Swoppits – cowboys on horseback which had interchangeable parts – but at 7/6d each it was an endless wait to buy the second one to start swopping the bits with. The one I really wanted was the

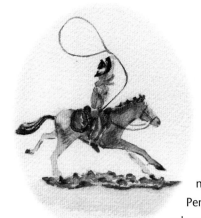

covered wagon with two horses but before I saved the £3/17/6d I began to get interested in buying records. These cost 6/8d a single (or 45s as we called them) so one a month was possible and I could cycle down to the music shop in The Link, near to the Penny Farthing bike shop. This shop was where Daddy would later be persuaded to buy my blue racing bike from – I'd window-shopped there until the glass had nearly worn away.

I also had to buy rabbit food out of my pocket money and that shop was also down The Link. My rabbit food visits were a bit more of a challenge though. I had to endure the whole procedure without the faintest squirm or hint of a giggle because Daddy said that it would be really cruel to laugh at the poor man, who was also one of Daddy's clients. The poor man had what Daddy called a "tick" but what I called an 'a-chuf-wheeeeeey' because that's what he would suddenly say as he uncontrollably threw his arms up in the air with his hilarious sneezing noise. On one particular shopping visit, he shuffled over to the bin of rabbit food and with a little trowel, slowly began scooping oats and maize into the large brown paper bag. Then, it seemed that he froze – and then I froze as the 'a-chuf' warning came. On cue, he violently flung out his arm and the whole shovel-full of little grains flew up into the air with a deliciously long *wheeeeeeeeeeeey*. I tried so

hard to look discreetly the other way but then the upwardly mobile little grains began their descent and landed like a hail of bullets, firstly over all the metal hardware and then the noisy bare floorboards. A little tremor began trembling into a little titter as I struggled to control my erupting laughter. How much longer could I hold this imminent explosion in? Holding my breath I turned pleadingly to the other man behind the counter as little pieces of flaked maize and rolled oats landed on his bald pink head. "That'll be 2/6d please," he said without twitching a muscle as a little piece of flaked maize slipped down his stony face. And that was it . . .
I only just made it out of the door.

Sunday is Fun Day

Although this was meant to be the beginning of an exciting new decade when we were all supposed to be embarking on a fresh, modern approach to life, Sundays remained well behind in the Fifties. Many families attended church in the morning. Every parish church rang its distinct peel of bells and I could count at least seven different churches ringing from our house. The people who had moved to our new houses from older ones in the town still attended their old churches, so best-coated-and-hatted families flurried off in different directions in their Sunday Best. Our 'nexdoor' neighbour took a long string of beads with her which I thought was being unnecessarily glamorous for a church service. The service I enjoyed the most was when the Salvation Army brought all their shiny instruments and played really loud hymns on our corner. You didn't have to dress up and you didn't have to sit still through all that grown-up speaking. And you could sing as loud as you felt like because however big the crowd, we could never drown all that brassy noise.

After that rousing morning, the afternoon was boringly quiet on our estate. Most people stayed in their Sunday Best all day. Very few children were allowed to play out in the streets or commons, just in their gardens, and only smartly dressed relations ever called at the door. Shops were closed and no-one except doctors and nurses and newspaper-boys went to work on Sundays.

Sundays were our family days, which we spent going out together. We were expected to dress up smartly for our outings and my parents still frowned upon little girls who went out wearing jeans or trousers because they were strictly play-clothes and NOT for Sundays. That took the edge off the day's enjoyment because how could you possibly pretend to be a cowboy galloping over the hills if you had to wear a silly dress or hefty woollen coat?

Our first Sunday outings in this new place were to explore the hills and countryside. Now that my sister had dispensed with her pushchair there were no limits to where we could go and out we went in all weathers to return with chapped legs where the wind had bitten into the soft pink flesh under our skirts. "Mummy I've got chaps!" I would wail, pleading for some jeans.

Eventually, after a particularly painful pink-legged outing, Daddy cut up a pair of his old trousers and made us each a warm pair from them. We really needed them that winter because it was the snowiest of my whole life. We still had to wear our best coats on top though – not something a cowboy would have done, I'm sure.

The first blizzard began on a Sunday, after a crisp, frosty Christmas when my sister scooted her new red Triang scooter to the phone box with us to wish Granny a Happy Christmas and say, "Thank you" for the very sensible presents. We hadn't got our own telephone yet because Daddy said the list was as long as his arm. I thought he meant the list of telephone numbers we might ring and waste money on. My great aunt had rung too many people and was "cut off" but I never found out which bit of her they chopped off. Anyway, by the time we got home the crispy golden morning had turned grey and

cold and giant feathery snowflakes began floating gently down.

"That'll blow the cobwebs away!" Mummy said as the wind began to howl. The wind blew so hard it blew the snow right back up into the sky again and blew the fireplace smoke into the room and made Mummy cross because it spoilt the nice Christmassy smells. It blew for three days until the snow on the lamp-post was as big as the whole lamp itself but then the cold wind stopped and we went out for a walk in the dark as a special treat. We blew our own cobwebs away, having been cooped up for three whole days.

The snow didn't begin to melt at all and only people who walked to work or school could go back after the holiday because the roads were still blocked deep with snow. Some silly people tried to drive their cars up the hill but they stopped and couldn't stop sliding

back down in a wiggly pattern so we had to stay safe in the garden at first. Then one night it froze really hard and a few cleverer cars managed to drive right up the hill but that just packed the snow into a perfect ski-run. All the cars had to put chains on their wheels after that, or just stay at home.

Daddy couldn't get all the way to his office because it was right over the river and he said some very silly people who couldn't drive properly had skidded and blocked the bridge. I was pleased because, instead, he made us a sledge in the garage and polished the runners smooth and shiny. Daddy knew all about those sorts of things. He liked doing that much better than wearing the suit Granny liked him to wear at his office.

Smart red shop sledges, home-made wooden ones and a few envied people on skis flocked to the slopes on The Common. Everyone joined in the fun and made friends with everyone else and they all kept saying, even to strangers, "This is Once-in-a-Lifetime Snow and we MUST enjoy it while we can."

Now I had lots of friends from all over the town and didn't have to worry about fitting in on our new estate. The snow stayed on the ground until March, when little clean patches of emerald grass began to grow through the shrinking snow, looking like the pattern on the cows in the meadow.

Other Sundays were spent in the hills exploring new valleys and peaks. I ignored Mummy's plea of, "Don't go near The Edge – it will grab your legs and pull them over the side!" because I knew The Edge was more friendly than that. Once we climbed right to the top of the tallest hill – even my little sister managed the steep climb – and right at the very top was a little wooden café selling tea and milk and slabs of very nice fruitcake. Daddy said you could see Wales from up there. I couldn't even see the sea, let alone any whales.

Mummy's favourite place was another common with a big fishing lake. Mummy liked it there because it was flat and none of us could be pulled off The Edge. We always had to walk away from the lake, though, so we wouldn't have our legs pulled in there either. Some Big Girls lived on the side of that common in a white house with three stables. They galloped their ponies all over that golden common like cowboys out on the range. How I wished I could be them.

When we got home on Sundays, Daddy stoked up the fire, made the Mock Crab sandwiches for tea and we'd watch whatever children's serial was on television. *The Secret Garden*, *The Railway Children*, *Oliver Twist* or *The Story of the Treasure Seekers* with my heroes, the Bastable children – all compelling me to read the real books and enter the classic reading world like no schoolteacher ever managed to do. Then as the evening drew dimly in, thoughts turned glumly towards Monday with bath-and-hairwash and early-to-bed – with Friday afternoon a very far-away feeling.

There's Snow Snow There

One cold Sunday in winter, Daddy announced cheerfully that he was taking us for a special treat. We were going to have lunch at the Winter Gardens.

Wow! What wonderful thoughts spun around in my head. A Winter Garden MUST have snow – and twinkly branches sparkling with light, silver sleighs pulled by jingle-belled white ponies and maybe, even Father Christmas at the picnic. I couldn't wait.

When we first arrived, I was mildly disappointed but as Daddy was still excited I kept it to myself so as not to spoil it for him. However, look at it from my point of view. The Winter Gardens turned out to be just "up town". And they were INDOORS (?!) so NO SNOW. You weren't allowed to run about. And the only trees were palms in pots. You definitely couldn't climb THEM!

Lunch wasn't too bad, even though it wasn't a proper picnic because there were tables and white-pinnied waitresses you had to speak

slowly edging back indoors again though and sure enough we soon entered a huge dimly lit, thickly carpeted room with rows and rows of chairs sloping down to some giant velvet red curtains. Everyone sat watching them, chatting excitedly. They must be waiting for the curtains to be opened so they could see the snowy, sparkly winter garden outside! I tried to sit still as I'd been told but the seat was too high and if I sat right on top of the little ledge, it tried to tip me off. So I just stood.

I waited and waited and fidgeted, eagerly anticipating the snow scene behind the curtains. I hoped they would let us play out there and not just look through the big window.

At long last, the curtain opened and everyone clapped and cheered . . . but where was my magic Winter Garden? All I could see was lots of people dressed up in frilly frocks, dancing around and singing about Cinderella!

My tired legs began to ache as the dark afternoon got worse and worse. Firstly, they got the Cinderella story all wrong. Then they kept interrupting the story to sing really silly songs. Then the people watching did something REALLY naughty and started shouting at poor Buttons, who'd only lost something behind him after all. Then, 'worstest' of all, they started arguing with the Ugly Sisters, saying they DID hide the slipper. It was true because they had – but still extremely rude and I went very red and hid my face away from the whole embarrassing episode. It was the worst special treat ever – except perhaps for Billy Smart's Circus where a man tied up a poor old lady and threw knives at her.

politely to. I did like the blackcurrant pie and thick yellow custard though – and Mummy was enjoying not having to cook so I didn't ask about the sparkly garden. Then, just as we were about to leave, Daddy said there was another treat and I thought that it MUST be the snowy sparkly Winter Garden this time so followed him bouncily outside where we joined a long queue. Mysteriously, we seemed to be

Rabbit Rabbit Rabbit

We were taken on another special treat, this time in a very wet summer. We were allowed the whole day off school to go to the Three Counties Show. I didn't know quite what to expect after the anti-climax of previous treats but everyone else seemed excited and we climbed to the top of the hills to watch the preparations in the huge field below. All I could make out were rows and rows of white tents and lots of tiny tractors trundling around, making miniature mud-tracks in the browning grass.

When we finally got there it was like an adventure playground because you had to walk along straw bales and narrow wooden planks so as not to fall in the squidgy mud beneath. That bit was fun but my little sister couldn't walk along these so Mummy took her to a special tent where small children were allowed to play. I wasn't small enough so I had to go with Daddy, who needed to visit all his 'Surance Clients'.

This too was fun at first because they all gave me biscuits and one tent was right next to the Main Ring. I was allowed to sit on top of the fence at the front, watching all the cattle and horses and pretending I was a cowboy on a ranch. After that tent, the visits got a little tedious because the grown-ups just talked and talked and drank grown-up drinks until they laughed too loudly and my ears and legs ached with boredom.

"Come on, we're going to see my Rabbit Man now," chivvied Daddy, tipping his grown-up drink into a potted geranium. "Perhaps we can buy some food for your rabbit."

The Rabbit Man was wearing a very furry white waistcoat. He stood in front of a low pen full of white rabbits which children were allowed to stroke. Down one side of his tent was a row of less fortunate rabbits crammed into small wire cages – and down the other side there were some uninteresting trays of pink meat.

"Do you like rabbit?" he bent down and asked me.

"I love rabbits," I answered shyly then turned to Daddy and asked, "Can we buy some food?"

The rabbit man seemed delighted and turned and pointed to his trays of pink meat,

"What would you like?"

I thought he was rather a stupid man because everyone knows that rabbits don't eat meat.

"Rolled oats," I answered blankly and he roared with laughter.

"You'll turn into a rabbit if you eat those! Here, I've got just the thing for you – it's a lucky charm so you might be able to use its magic to turn yourself into a rabbit!"

He handed me a tiny white rabbit's foot with a horrid little hook and chain where the poor rabbit's leg should have been. I stroked the little dead foot and quietly cried and Daddy was given another drink – which he slowly tipped out in the mud when the nasty rabbit man was busy laughing.

Brownie Points

One day a boy knocked on the door and said, "Bob-a-Job?" and Mummy let him straight in even though we didn't know him. Then she got out all our shoes for him to clean, which was also very strange because that was Daddy's job.

The boy was dressed in a green jumper with badges sewn on untidily, and a green cap, which he forgot to take off when he came indoors, and long brown socks with little green ribbons dangling from the garters. The best bit of all though was his neckerchief that was fastened round his neck just like a cowboy and I suddenly wanted one like that very badly. I stared longingly at it until Mummy gave him a shilling and he gave her a sticker with a tick on. The sticker was to go in the window to stop other little green boys knocking and being a nuisance.

"Can I have a cowboy scarf?" I pleaded.

"He's not a cowboy, he's a Cub Scout. That's what they wear."

"Please can I be a Cub Scout?"

"You can be a girl cub. They're called Brownies," I was told and I pictured a cuddly brown bear-cub.

A Big Girl came round a few weeks later and gave me her old Brownie uniform. She said she was soon "flying up" but I didn't ask where in case she meant she was dying and flying up to heaven. When she unpacked it and showed it to me I was hugely disappointed. Firstly, it was a DRESS – so how could you play cowboys in that? And then the Brownie neckerchief was worn folded neatly in a tie, not at all like a cowboy neckerchief.

I said I didn't want to be a Brownie any more, thank you and cried. Mummy, however, said I HAD to go and be a Brownie because someone had gone to a lot of trouble to find two places so that me and my friend could go together. It was at an old school in the old brick part of town and a long way to walk but Mummy said we should be very grateful – "and pleased".

Things didn't start too well because when we arrived a naughty girl at the school gate shouted, "This ent your school!" and slapped me on the face. So I went in with a red hand-shape imprinted on my cheek and all the little Brownie faces stared. Then I noticed with horror

a giant red-spotted toadstool growing in the middle of the room as I knew they were VERY poisonous and you must NEVER go near them. A lady in blue who said she was called Brown Owl (which I rather doubted) then made all the Brownies hold hands and dance around it, singing,

We're the Brownies, Here's our Aim,
Lend a Hand and Play the Game.

But she seemed to forget all about the Game and told us to go into our SIX corners. That made me doubt her even more because even I knew the room only had FOUR corners.

The six children in my corner were called Sprites and my Sixer told us what to do next. Two girls had to tie knots in pieces of string around chairs and another had to learn to walk on flowerpots right across the room without putting her feet on the ground. I hoped

I would be doing that because it looked fun and might be a really useful skill to have one day. Instead, I had to sit still and learn the Brownie Law and Promise all off by heart. I must have looked a bit fed up about it because the owl lady came over and said, "It's Brownie Revels in the woods on Saturday, you'll enjoy that I'm sure."
I wasn't sure.

Every Brownie Pack in the neighbourhood went to Revels. However, just me and my friend went from our pack because all the others, who went to a different school, had a school trip. Hundreds of unknown Brownie faces surrounded us as we massed in a clearing in the woods of a large country estate. Again, we encircled another giant, poisonous, red toadstool, which I was sure was going to make me die painfully. After a failed attempt to get the herd of Brownies to all dance around it without bumping, another Brown Owl told us all we were going to try and find our way back to Base Camp following tracking signs. That sounded a bit more interesting as I imagined the base camp having colourful wigwams and piebald ponies, but then she said that on the way back we must find all the things we could eat or drink if we ever got lost in the woods. After that I was worried that we would indeed get lost.

Each pack was given a screw-top

jam-jar but when the Brown Owl looked at us she said it was rather a waste of a big jar for just two people. In the end she very reluctantly handed us a tiny fish-paste jar.

As soon as she blew her whistle, one Brownie squealed, "Tracks!" and the whole herd followed, disappearing into the woods.

I knew that wasn't the way we had come, so led my friend in the opposite direction looking for the food and drink on our way.

"There's wild garlic!" I exclaimed but knew I shouldn't pick wild flowers, ". . . and mushrooms, look!" but we knew never to pick them either in case they were poisonous toadstools. Then, as we crossed over a little stream, we collected some water and caught some little water-shrimps in our tiny jar but poured them back when we felt sorry for them cramped in that small space.

We had just resigned ourselves to being hopelessly lost and nearing starvation, when a long low building loomed up before us and despite the danger of maybe meeting The Three Bears inside, we peeped cautiously around the open door.

Inside was a long table stacked high with plates of sandwiches, cakes and orange squash.

"THIS must be the food and drink for when you are lost!" my friend exclaimed.

"Are we lost?" I asked and before she replied we tucked in and ate all the cakes and sandwiches we could manage, finishing off with several cups of squash. Feeling in need of a little fresh air after that, we wandered outside and sat beneath the cool leaves at the wood's edge.

After a while, the other Brownies began to arrive carrying an array of wild garlic, nuts, mushrooms and jam-jars swimming with shrimps. Brown Owl ticked off a huge sheet and awarded points per portion and prizes to the winners. Our pack got no points at all but she said it was quite a good try for only two of us and we were, somehow, the first to arrive back, so "Well done". She gave us one little I-Spy book for our whole pack. After that we all sang our Brownie song – this time without trying to dance around a toadstool – and Brown Owl announced that we could all go into the hut and have just ONE cake and ONE sandwich each with a SMALL cup of squash. . . Ooops.

Sink or Swim

In the detached house next to us lived two Big Girls who I thought must be very, very clever because they played the piano and wore straw hats to school. They saw me as a worthy recipient of their wisdom and were constantly offering to introduce me to "educational" and "cultural" clubs like drama or singing groups. However, as any kind of performance in public was my ultimate worst nightmare, I stubbornly rebuffed their kind invitations. Even when they attempted to give me private piano lessons, in their front room, I was too frightened to go beyond performing "thumb on middle C" – just in case anyone was listening in the next room.

Ultimately frustrated into cunning plans to coerce me into co-operation, they offered to take me swimming. I keenly accepted because I had recently ventured right out to "third wave deep" in the sea with feet off the bottom (largely because it was stony) so I knew I was now a Very Good Swimmer and boldly told them so. When they said we would WALK there though, I began to lack confidence in their supposed wisdom because even I knew the sea was a very long way from our homes and it would probably get dark before we even got there. That was scary.

When we finally arrived at our destination, I began to wonder if I'd been brought instead to some kind of punishment place (like the home where the naughty boys went to do digging and hoe weeds) because you had to enter through some hard metal turnstiles into a freezing cold, concrete room full of cells and metal crates. I stood there stupified, hoping either for heroic rescue or for swift awakening from this horrible nightmare, but the Big Girls gently ushered me into one of these cells telling me to get changed and put my clothes and shoes into the wire crate. I obeyed and stood in the cell for ages and ages wondering how long I'd have to remain in prison, until one of the girls reached in and grabbed my hand.

"Come on slow-coach, we've swum two lengths already!" and she took my crate of clothes and shoes to a girl behind a tall counter. I hoped the girl would give them back one day because my sandals were brand new and I mustn't grow out of them before they were worn out or I might not be allowed red ones again. The girl behind the tall counter gave me a numbered rubber band and my big friend placed it round my wrist. At first I thought it was a play-watch from a cracker but then resigned myself to the fact that it was the thing they put on your wrist before you had your adenoids out. Well, they couldn't take mine out again. Perhaps this time they were taking my tonsils out.

"Come on, this is meant to be fun!" my big friend giggled and led me out into the blinding sunlight of the town lido. A gigantic blue pool full of splashing and squealing children stretched before us and my two big friends immediately ran ahead and dived into the dark blue water at the far end. They again left me alone and scared, this time amongst a sea of laughing, leering faces.

"Get in then!" shoved one girl whose way I was blocking. Consequently I was rather unwillingly introduced to the menacing pale-blue water at the shallow end. I gripped tightly with both hands on the cold metal rail, turning my back on the slashing water which smelt like lavatory cleaner and stung my eyes.

"Come on, it's not at all cold!" my big friend beckoned but I stubbornly refused to budge. This wasn't at all like the cool, salt-tasting sea-water which firmly floated you upwards and rocked you gently in its waves. This nasty smelling, stinging, blue warm stuff was going to try to drown me. Try as they did all afternoon to prise my hands off the rail, there I remained shivering and squirming for the rest of their special treat.

My piano lessons never resumed and the Big Girls eventually found more willing pupils to impart their wisdom to. Unfortunately for me though, the swimming nightmare did resume. My headteacher announced that the Juniors would all be attending weekly swimming lessons. We were to go by coach, which was really exciting as most of us hadn't ridden on a coach before and it helped to block out the fear of my fate at the end of the journey. The coach was a bit like a bus but it had thick padded carpets on its extra-springy seats which made them great to bounce up and down on. Each seat had an ashtray which swiftly swung shut and bit your fingers with a loud snap. That seemed to annoy the driver for some reason but we knew he would never really be allowed to throw us off the coach and make us walk. He should have cleaned out the ashtrays if he didn't want ash all over the seats. The seats were higher up than on buses so you could see out of the windows when you got bored of bouncing.

"That's MY house!" children squealed in turn as their homes magically appeared throughout the journey up to town.

"That's where my dad works, look!"

"There's my mum shopping!"

"Look, there's my mum with your dad!"

Soon we got to the leafy part of town where the bigger houses were and nobody's home was and the coach stopped by the park where the tall evergreens surrounded the swimming pool. When we first arrived, I thought it was a different place because there were no screaming crowds and the blue water was still and smooth as glass. It actually looked quite inviting. Once in the changing rooms though, I remembered the cold cells and crates and repeated the strange routine my big friends had shown me. After waiting an age by the tall empty counter for the absent girl to take my clothes and give me a rubber band, my teacher stormed in from the pool, took my clothes back to my cell and rebuked me for wasting time. You could never win with big people.

Everyone was lined up and we had to say how far we could swim. The ones who said they couldn't swim had to get in the shallow end by the safe metal rail. Some could swim a bit so they went in the middle bit where they could only just touch the bottom on tip-toe. The rest proudly said they had 'Seasin Ticks' and they got sent to the dark blue deep water at the far end. I definitely didn't want EVER to go there and made a mental note never to have a 'Seasin Tick'. I told them that I could only swim in the sea with a rubber ring and holding Daddy's hand – which was a tiny bit of a fib but secured my place in the safe shallow end.

Following this selection process, the consequential new social ranking was a revelation to us and had a lasting positive effect back at school. Each declaration of 'swimability' brought either squeals of surprise and delight, or gasps of horror. Our first joy was when the big class bully squirmed, "Please don't make me get in, I'm scared of water!" and then our star sportsman visibly shrank before us when he timidly muttered, "...I can't swim".

Conversely, two formerly teased large, waddly girls proudly

The Sad, Hatless T. Pratley

There were scores of boarding schools in town, occupying the huge houses and hotels from the town's spa legacy. I used to think that boarding schools were places for the poor – like in *Oliver Twist*. This belief arose initially because whilst walking up to town with Mummy, we saw a boy arrive at his school carrying a small suitcase and squashing a teddy under his arm.

"Poor little thing," Mummy said and I looked at the squashed teddy and agreed.

"What's in his suitcase?" I asked and she answered sadly,

"All his things."

Then I knew she must have meant the BOY was a poor little thing, not the teddy, because he must have been very poor indeed if he could get ALL his things into that small suitcase.

Once we went carol singing at a boarding school. It was by mistake really because we thought it was just a great big house. All the girls in there were poor too. They invited us in and sat in their dressing gowns on a bare wooden staircase, listening patiently to our dubious dulcet tones. After we'd run out of carols, one girl came forward and said, "We've put all our money together for you but we haven't a lot left as it's nearly Christmas," and she rather shamefully slid a few pence

showed their prowess by diving into the deep end and racing each other along two lengths, interspersed with superb "racing turns". Even little Tommy Twit proved our preconceptions wrong by backward somersaulting off the diving board – although he had failed to ensure there was no-one underneath first, rather confirming his original nickname. It was difficult after that, though, for anyone to meet approval by bullying those previously bullied children or to blindly admire the former heroes. I think we learnt more from that lesson than we did from the actual swimming lessons.

The best revelation of all to me though was the discovery that my headteacher, who'd constantly referred to me as a "Silly Little Girl" was actually rather a "silly little man" himself. In either a moment of sheer madness, or vanity brought about by prancing around in tight swimwear, he dived into the shallow baby pool and consequently sliced all the skin off his nose. We all wanted that scar to last forever because for as long as its rosy crust crowned his nose, his sneery name-calling ceased.

into our tin. Then a white-aproned lady in the dining room called us all in, cooing, "Supper-time, gals!" but all they were given was cocoa in old tin mugs. We, on the other hand, were offered iced buns and a whole plate of biscuits.

On our way out we counted all the funny brown hats on the cloakroom pegs. You could always tell who in town went to boarding schools because they all had to wear hats. My friend introduced me to a game involving these hats. On the last day of our holidays she took me to the bridge overlooking the railway station where the College girls were arriving for start of term. It seemed to be a tradition for them to all wave their felt hats out of the train windows as it approached and inevitably one hat would get snatched by the wind and squashed under the greasy carriage wheels. When the train doors flung open and the squealing mass of maroon girls emerged, the game was "Spot the Hatless One" – a bit like *Where's Wally*. The hatless one was usually the girl in floods of tears. You had to be quick, though, for all the girls would magically disappear from the platform into a silent nowhere. We thought they must have a secret underground passageway into the school across the road, so we went down and jumped on all the stone slabs on the platform, listening for a hollow one. We couldn't make any of them open though and the guard got annoyed and asked us to, "Leave please, if you would", which we did.

The Boys' College pupils wore flat straw boaters with ribbons around, which I thought rather odd for boys. I knew they must have been poor too because the music shop had little booths where you could listen to records if you didn't have enough money to buy them and on Saturdays the booths were always full of poor College boys. They used to take their hats off to listen and then forget and leave them behind in the booths. The shopkeeper always had a huge pile of left-behind hats on his counter. Once, my friend saw a boy leave the shop with his boater still in the booth and being much bolder than I was, she ran out into the street waving his hat. She looked inside it for his name and shouted,

"T. Pratley, I've got your hat!" and a red-faced T. Pratley spuffled out from the curious crowd,

"Thank you SO much," he sighed with relief, "they NEVER let you out if you don't have a hat!".

After that I always felt sorry for all those hatless boys who would never, ever be let out of school again.

Training for the Future

My primary school was brand new and smelt of polish and pencils. It was built right at the start of the Sixties and had tried to be very modern in design but I think it tried too hard. The interior of the building was a mix of different designs and the patterns and colours didn't match together at all. Outside looked quite nice though.

Daddy said 'The Arkatec' had drawn a pop-art squiggle on the plans for the bare end-wall but, luckily, the builders thought it was meant to be a horse and made a giant blue rearing horse to hang there. This big blue rearing horse then became our school badge.

Our brand new school was meant for all the children on the new estate but as the house-building was nowhere near finished, children from other schools were allowed to come and fill it up. It started with just 60 children from 4 to 11 years old, in three classes. Although I was only seven, I was therefore in the top class and inevitably the youngest and smallest. We each sat in our own desk in formal lines, quite unlike the friendly family tables of my Infants' school. No-one sat beside me and there was a Big Boy behind me and another in front. As I didn't like the look of either, I didn't speak to anyone at all for the first term. As my shy apprehension was taken to mean "dullness", I was taken out daily with two older children for Remedial Maths. Unaware of the stigma this gave me in the eyes of the other children, these lessons became the highlight of my day because they took place in the staff-room and that room overlooked the field in which the busy Hereford to Paddington railway line ran. My excitement and expectation for these lessons was almost overwhelming and completely baffled The Head.

I always made sure I was first to arrive in the room so I could get the chair opposite the huge window and then one hour of bliss would roll by, as train after train puffed past – because this was still the age of steam.

The Head would give us a card with a hook and hold up a ladder of numbers, then ask us a sum. We were supposed to count up or down the ladder and hang the card on the answer.

I failed to do this most of the time, largely because as soon as he asked a question the gentle *huff-puff* of a steam engine began its approach from the distant station and I couldn't bear to take my eyes away from that splendid sight until the last carriage had passed behind the trees. *Te-dum-te-dum, te-dum-te-dum.*

I soon got to know the timetable and could look away at the clock whilst pretending to count until I just HAD to look at the railway. Once a non-timetabled train took me by surprise just as I was asked to add 3 onto 7. It was drawing 22 trucks towards the bigger station. I hurriedly hooked my answer on the number 10 but it fell onto the floor and I took a while finding it under the table. In the midst of my search, I heard the train returning and leapt back to my seat – same 0-6-0 tank-engine pulling coal-trucks – but only 17 trucks. What had happened to the other five trucks? I hastily threw my answer card onto the number 10 hook so I could count the trucks again but it landed carelessly on the nine.

"You Silly Girl!" announced The Head, "Can't you even do 7+3?"

Some of the finest Great Western steam engines passed by on that line from the grand 4-6-0 green Castle Class expresses to the little black tank engines. Our generation was the last to have the privilege of seeing them at work. Unfortunately for me this daily privilege halted when we had to work in a different room one day and without this wonderful distraction I got all my answers right and was allowed back into the mainstream maths lessons. It still didn't stop The Head calling me "A Silly Little Girl" though.

It was difficult being "new". I felt as if I'd only just begun to fit in at my Infants' school, and now it was all confusing again, especially with strange children arriving all the time. They all wore the different uniforms of their old schools at first to "wear them out" before buying our smart new French Blue and Silver Grey one.

Perhaps this array of uniforms confused Mummy too because she finally bought me the two powder blue blouses which I should have worn at my previous Infants' school. She bought them because they were Viyella. Mummy had a little snooty sort of thing about Viyella clothes. I just found them very itchy. Unfortunately the blouses at this school were supposed to be white and so I got left out of the "white-blouse-set" right from the start.

Being selected for the Remedial Maths class hadn't helped my social standing either and making friends in the playground was at first problematic. A not-too-bright older boy, who was quietly avoided because of his threadbare clothes, immediately latched on to me as a friendless fellow-sufferer. As he was readily willing to play cowboys, or outlaws, or indeed play ANYTHING if it meant having a friend, I happily joined him but it wasn't long before this unusual friendship got us both into a pickle.

"Play Robin 'ood?" was his usual greeting and as he'd already gathered two balaclava-ed infants to play the Sheriff's men it seemed a possible good game.

"Only if I can be Robin Hood," I bargained, because he would definitely have had the best horse. The balaclava-ed infants, completely overawed by any Big Boy who deigned to ask them to play, consequently venerated any utterances he uttered. That was probably why they agreed so amicably to being taken prisoner and tied to the drainpipe behind the classroom by the belts of their navy gabardine macs. We knew Robin Hood was a kind man – he didn't hurt his prisoners, he just robbed them – so we just left them there whilst we robbed some more rich and found some poor recipients, accompanied by (and in galloping time to) the television theme-tune,

> *Robin Hood, Robin Hood, riding through the glen,*
> *Robin Hood, Robin Hood, with his band of men,*
> *Feared by the bad, loved by the good,*
> *Robin Hood . . . Robin Hood . . . Robin Hood.*

Unfortunately, while we were away robbing the rich, the school bell rang and, unable to untie their belts, the balaclava-ed infants just pulled and pulled frantically thus tightening their belts even more. By the time we answered their screams, the playground had emptied – all except for the pink-coated playground supervisor.

I had not, at this stage of my education, realised the importance of being on the right side of Pink Playground Ladies. They didn't behave in quite the same way as normal grown-ups, often going completely over the top in reaction to the mildest of mishaps. This Pink Playground Supervisor said sternly,

"You are hideous thugs and bullies!" (which was not true because

Robin Hood was one of the "goodies" and feared only by the bad).
Then she announced, "You are NOT allowed to go anywhere near
those infants again. EVER!" which was going to be rather tricky in
our small crowded playground.

"Play nex playtime?" the undaunted Big Boy chirped, as we ran
into class to be told off yet again for being late, which wasn't really
our fault as we'd only been trying to rescue the prisoners from the
Pink Playground Lady.

Next playtime we found two different over-awed and willing
captives but we decided to play "Cowboys-and-Indians" this time as
they had no balaclavas on. Instead they were wearing brand-new
smart school scarves in our very exclusive French Blue and Silver Grey
stripe, so we used these to tie them to the totem pole drainpipe and
pretended to light a fire under their feet. After a good deal of tugging
and stretching at bell-time, the prisoners were eventually released
only to discover their smart new scarves had trebled in length and
shrunk to just inches in width, dangling apologetically along the wet
playground as they ran in.

After that Mummy and Daddy had to go into school and see my
class teacher about why I was not making Suitable Playground
Relationships. I couldn't understand why they thought we'd been
playing 'Relays-and-Ships' when it was quite obviously "Cowboys-
and-Indians".

Sometimes grown-ups are quite silly.

The Exam That Didn't Really Matter

As more classrooms were completed we moved into the grown-up
two-storey part of the school. It smelt all new and varnishy again and
our shoes stuck to the new non-slip floor when we tried to slip on it.
These new classrooms shared their own proper library which to me was
absolute bliss. I read methodically through all the crisp white pages
of the shiny new books and lost myself in Dolphins and Puffins and
then the Ladybird Nature series enticingly and delightfully illustrated
by a man called Tunnicliffe. It gave a huge boost to my reading powers
and art appreciation – but again not to my social skills as I hid myself
away, lost in books.

With a wide age-range to cater for, the class teacher would
concentrate the formal lessons on the older children. This left me time
to myself giving me freedom to read or write pages of endless stories
until my hand ached too much to write on. Then, I would eavesdrop
on the top Juniors' English lessons (especially when I was supposed

to be doing maths exercises). I soon learnt all the fascinating facts and features of punctuation and grammar and useless-but-interesting facts, like lots of geese being called a "gaggle". I thought that might come in very useful one day.

As a consequence of that and of missing out on "place-value" lessons whilst train-spotting, my maths education fell seriously behind and never really caught up. I was just a "Silly Little Girl" who couldn't do maths, so I just sat and did nothing.

The Head continued to call me "A Silly Little Girl" until halfway through the top Juniors when we all did a practice IQ test. After that test, my parents were told I could get into a Really Good Big School. I thought I would rather stay at this school, thank you.

All the top Juniors – except me and the Remedials – had been given homework books called 11+ Progress Papers; green for English, blue for maths and yellow for Intelligence ones. I hadn't questioned why I'd been left out because I didn't particularly want to do any homework. After the practice IQ test though, The Head gave me those three books too – but I was a long, long way behind by then and had to work through them on my own.

The English was easy and I romped through the little comprehensions and punctuations in a week, wishing there was another book. The IQ papers were easy too because all you had to do was match the patterns in shapes, or say which way up they'd turned. However, the maths papers were like a foreign language to me so I didn't do them at all. I pretended I'd lost the book when The Head asked to mark it. Unfortunately he still wanted to know how much I'd learnt so he asked me a question – in front of the WHOLE CLASS.

"What's the difference between 2 and 7?" he asked.

"They're both the same," I answered shyly after long consideration. The Head looked angrily back.

"How on earth can they be the same?" he ridiculed and the class tittered nervously.

"Because they are both blue," I answered confidently but as there were now several sniggers amongst my classmates I declined the invitation to explain further.

"You Silly Little Girl," sneered The Head and moved on to his clever pupils.

At playtime afterwards, the pretty ginger-haired girl from the bungalow by the railway (who I had previously hated for having her bungalow built on our train-spotting meadow) approached me.

"I know why you said that. But MY 2 is a greeny blue and 7 is ice-blue so I don't think I wouldn't have said they were exactly the same."

After that I liked her a little more and played with her on the climbing frame. She was obviously quite clever but just couldn't do maths, which was just like me. And she did live in the best train-spotting field and might ask me to tea one day.

I didn't know then, that not everyone thinks in colours

like that or that the condition we had was called synaesthesia. I only realise now, 50 years on, how it might have contributed to our difficulties with numbers.

As our 11+ Selection Exam drew near, school conversations involving this extremely important, but rather distant day, dramatically and mysteriously metamorphosed. Having cajoled and coaxed us meticulously through all the practice papers, with instructions on how to read the questions, check your answers and even how to turn over the pages, The Head suddenly announced that it WASN'T really a very important exam at all.

"There is no need to worry about it at all," he said.

Until he said that, it hadn't really occurred to us to worry anyway. Then our class teacher sent all the younger children out and gave us a little speech "all to ourselves" as a "special day" was approaching. He then said that it wasn't really a special day at all and we just had to work as normal – and whatever school we went to in the end would be the best one for us. So it was nothing to worry about. That made us all worry that we WEREN'T worried about it and our carefree playground chatter took on a new sinister tone.

"My dad's buying me a new bike if I pass," boasted Jon and we were so envious because we all knew he would pass easily.

"My mum and dad are giving me money," another gloated and we enviously asked how much money and wondered if we could work on our own parents for a reward. But then when Faye said she'd be getting some new shoes as her reward we all looked sorrowfully down at her tatty ones – because we knew she wouldn't pass in a million years.

"My dad says it's the Most Important Exam We'll Ever Take. It will affect the WHOLE of the rest of our lives," the doctor's son solemnly stated. Then I began to wish I had not pretended to lose my blue Progress Papers in Mathematics. To make it worse, The Head then told me that my maths was "merely borderline' and that how I did on the maths paper would determine My WHOLE Future.
No pressure then.

The day came and went.

After it went we were all happy again. We could now do fun and interesting lessons like going to the meadow to search for 'bugs 'n' insecs' or go pond-dipping and laugh when posh Paula fell in the pond and had to go home and change her smelly black clothes. We learnt songs and sang together with lots of other schools at a huge music festival in a Big School conducted by Mr Benoy, who could get even the most unmusical voice to make a nice sound and enjoy it.

We all loved singing for him and he said we had raised the roof off and he would have to send for the builders. I looked up but couldn't see any gaps. After all the schools had sung together, each school sung their own chosen song and he helped them sing that better too – but he didn't help us with ours. That was because our Head had made us learn and recite a polite poem instead of a nice song because it was "good for our e-n-u-n-c-i-a-t-i-o-n". I really couldn't see why 'nungsiating' was better than enjoying a good sing and I think Mr Benoy agreed with me because when we'd finished he just coughed and said,

"Let's all finish with a good old rousing sea-shanty," and we all sang about drunken men in boats, as loudly as we wanted, and we linked arms and swayed – which OUR teachers NEVER let us do.

My highlight of the year was Inter-School Sports Day. It was always held at our school because we had a huge field big enough for a proper round relay track and a 100-yard straight. All the competing schools had pinned-on numbers and sat by the track on benches to watch and cheer. It was always a sunny day and the sun bounced back off the dry golden grass on the hills in a happy sort of way.

I crowned my final Junior school year by winning the 100 Yards Flat and the final leg of the 4 x 4 Relay, becoming a short-lived school heroine.

The Head didn't call me a "Silly Girl" that day. He didn't think I was a "Silly Girl" on the day I won the Brooke Bond Art Competition either, but cheekily made a speech about how good HIS school was at art. Just for those two days I was "A Very Talented Little Girl".

Then the 11+ results came out.

Even though I hadn't passed the 11+, Daddy bought me the blue racing bike from the bike-shop window to ride to my new school on, so that was the best thing about it all. Also, I wouldn't have to wear a silly black felt hat, which I was quite pleased about. Mummy felt quite sorry about the hat, although not so sorry as she was about me missing out on Elocution and Deportment lessons. In compensation, my little sister later emerged from the Grammar School very well 'elocuted' and nicely 'deported' in her smart black felt hat.

I was – and remain – grossly 'inelocuted' and 'undeported' to this day.